LESSON PLAN BOOK

Great Source Education Group
a Houghton Mifflin Company
Wilmington, Massachusetts

www.greatsource.com

AUTHORS

Jim Burke
Author

Burlingame High School, Burlingame, California
Jim Burke, author of *Reading Reminders: Tools, Tips, and Techniques* and *The English Teacher's Companion,* has taught high school English for 13 years. His most recent books, *Tools for Thought* and *Illuminating Texts: How to Teach Students to Read the World,* further explore reading and those strategies that can help all students succeed in high school. He was the recipient of the California Reading Association's Hall of Fame Award in 2001 and the Conference on English Leadership's Exemplary English Leadership Award in 2000. He currently serves on the National Board of Professional Teaching Standards for English Language Arts.

Ron Klemp
Contributing Author

Los Angeles Unified School District, Los Angeles, California
Ron Klemp is the Coordinator of Reading for the Los Angeles Unified School District. He has taught Reading, English, and Social Studies and was a middle school Dean of Discipline. He is also a coordinator/facilitator at the Secondary Practitioner Center, a professional development program in the Los Angeles Unified School District. He has been teaching at California State University, Cal Lutheran University, and National University.

Wendell Schwartz
Contributing Author

Adlai Stevenson High School, Lincolnshire, Illinois
Wendell Schwartz has been a teacher of English for 36 years. For the last 24 years he also has served as the Director of Communication Arts at Adlai Stevenson High School. He has taught gifted middle school students for the last 12 years, as well as teaching graduate-level courses for National Louis University in Evanston, Illinois.

Editorial: Developed by Nieman, Inc. with Phil LaLeike
Design: Ronan Design: Christine Ronan, Sean O'Neill, Maria Mariottini, Victoria Mullins
Illustrations: Mike McConnell

Printed in the United States of America
International Standard Book Number: 0-669-049504-2
1 2 3 4 5 6 7 8 9—MZ—08 07 06 05 04 03

READERS AND REVIEWERS

Dr. Leslie Adams
Division of Language
   Arts and Reading
Miami, FL

Ceci Aguilar
Telles Academy
El Paso, TX

Lynn Beale
Irvin High School
El Paso, TX

Jeannie Bosley
West Education
San Francisco, CA

John Brassil
Mt. Ararat High School
Topsham, ME

Doug Buehl
Madison East High School
Madison, WI

Maria Bunge
Austin High School
El Paso, TX

Roseanne Comfort
Westview High School
Portland, OR

Paula Congdon
Rockwood School District
Eureka, MO

Bonnie Davis
Education Park
St. Louis, MO

Lela DeToye
Southern Illinois University
Edwardsville, IL

Kathy Dorholt
New York Mills High School
New York Mills, MN

Steve Edwards
Central High School
Clearwater, FL

Lyla Fox
Loy Norrix High School
Kalamazoo, MI

Jodi Gardner
Assata High School
Milwaukee, WI

Karen Gibson
Appleton North
   High School
Appleton, WI

Laura Griffo
Jefferson Co. International
Irondale, AL

Carol Hallman
Ross Local School District
Hamilton, OH

Kerry Hansen
Dominican HS
Whitefish Bay, WI

Carol Sue Harless
DeKalb County School
   System
Stone Mountain, GA

Rebecca Hartman
Penn-Harris High School
Mishawaka, IN

Christine Heerlein
Rockwood Summit
   High School
Fenton, MO

Vicky Hoag
Fresno Co. Office of
   Education
Fresno, CA

Jack Hobbs
San Marcos High School
Santa Barbara, CA

Eileen Johnson
Edina Public Schools
Edina, MN

Laurel Key
Central High School
West Allis, WI

Michelle Knotts
Sinagua High School
Flagstaff, AZ

Kathleen Lask
Pattonville Senior
   High School
Maryland Heights, MO

Jean Lawson
Coronado High School
El Paso, TX

Jean Lifford
Dedham High School
Dedham, MA

Tom Lueschow
University of
   WI–Whitewater
Whitewater, WI

Maria Manning
Dade County Public Schools
Miami, FL

Jean-Marie Marlin
Mountain Brook High
   School
Birmingham, AL

Karen McMillan
Miami-Dade County Schools
Miami, FL

Judith Lynn Momirov
Buckeye Trail High School
Lore City, OH

Lisa Muller
Castle High School
Newburgh, IN

David P. Noskin
Adlai E. Stevenson
   High School
Lincolnshire, IL

Cheryl Nuciforo
Enlarged City School
   District of Troy
Troy, NY

Carolyn Novy
Chicago, IL

Rebecca Romine
Traverse City Central
   High School
Kewadin, MI

Jeannie Scott
Colorado Springs Dist. 11
Colorado Springs, CO

Susie Schneider
El Paso School District
El Paso, TX

Cathleen Search
Traverse City West
   High School
Traverse City, MI

Judy Smith
Rockwood School District
Eureka, MO

Leslie Somers
Miami-Dade Public Schools
Miami, FL

Sharon Straub
Joel E. Ferris High School
Spokane, WA

Michael Thompson
Minnesota Dept. of Children,
   Families, and Learning
Roseville, MN

Mary Ann Warnhoff
Eureka High School
Glendale, MO

Mary Weber
Waterford Kettering High
   School
Waterford, MI

Nancy Wilson
Gladstone High School
Gladstone, OR

Susan Wilson
South Orange
   Middle School
South Orange, NJ

Sandy Wojcik
Downers Grove High
   School South
Downers Grove, IL

Fred Wolff
Educational Consultant
Lee, NH

Table of Contents

Lesson Plan Book Overview

The *Lesson Plan Book* includes a suggested reading curriculum for each grade level, weekly and daily lesson plans, and professional articles.

Week at a Glance

The Weekly Plan shows **daily lessons** for the week.

Summary notes give a brief description of each lesson.

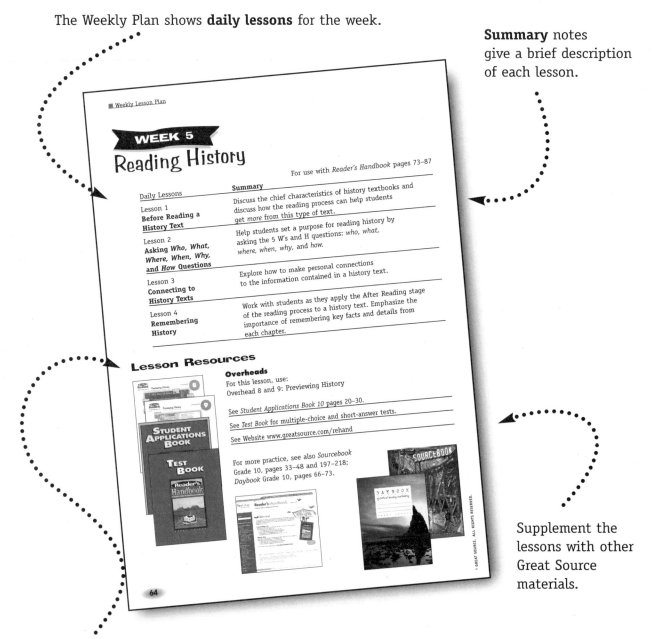

■ Weekly Lesson Plan

WEEK 5
Reading History

For use with *Reader's Handbook* pages 73–87

Daily Lessons	Summary
Lesson 1 **Before Reading a History Text**	Discuss the chief characteristics of history textbooks and discuss how the reading process can help students get *more* from this type of text.
Lesson 2 **Asking *Who, What, Where, When, Why,* and *How* Questions**	Help students set a purpose for reading history by asking the 5 W's and H questions: *who, what, where, when, why,* and *how.*
Lesson 3 **Connecting to History Texts**	Explore how to make personal connections to the information contained in a history text.
Lesson 4 **Remembering History**	Work with students as they apply the After Reading stage of the reading process to a history text. Emphasize the importance of remembering key facts and details from each chapter.

Lesson Resources

Overheads
For this lesson, use:
Overhead 8 and 9: Previewing History

See *Student Applications Book 10* pages 20–30.

See *Test Book* for multiple-choice and short-answer tests.

See Website www.greatsource.com/rehand

For more practice, see also *Sourcebook* Grade 10, pages 33–48 and 197–218; *Daybook* Grade 10, pages 66–73.

STUDENT APPLICATIONS BOOK

TEST BOOK

Reader's Handbook

SOURCEBOOK

DAYBOOK

64

Supplement the lessons with other Great Source materials.

The **Lesson Resources** show all of the other materials that accompany the lesson.

Lesson Plans

Each daily lesson begins with a **Goal**.

The **Teaching Focus** section gives background along with key instruction.

WEEK 5
Lesson 2

Asking Who, What, Where, When, Why, and How Questions

For use with *Reader's Handbook* pages 74–82

Goals

In this lesson, students learn how the 5 W's and H can provide a framework for reading history textbooks.

Teaching Focus

Background
Asking the 5 W's and H—*who, what, where, when, why,* and *how*—is a simple but highly effective way for students to establish a purpose for their reading and determine a focus for their note-taking. Explain to students that asking these questions throughout the reading helps to sustain their interest in the subject and to deepen their understanding. Show them how they can use two note-taking styles—Reporter's Notes and Key Word or Topic Notes—for history texts.

Instruction
Have volunteers imagine they are newspaper reporters who have traveled to Medina to write a profile on Muhammad. Have students list the questions they would ask Muhammad. Write the questions on the board in the style of Reporter's Notes. Lead students to see that the reporter's 5 W's and H are also useful for studying history.

Teaching Approach

Use of the Handbook
Have a volunteer read Set a Purpose on page 74 of the handbook. Then form small groups and have students work through pages 74–81. Visit each group to make sure that they understand the process of setting a purpose, previewing, and planning.

Extend the Handbook
Have students choose a chapter from their history textbooks to practice the Before Reading steps of setting a purpose, planning, and previewing.

Assessment
Ask students:
■ How can answering the 5 W's and H clarify your purpose for reading history?
■ How can the Before Reading steps and strategy of note-taking make you a more active reader?

67

The **Teaching Approach** shows how to use and extend the handbook with the lesson, as well as ways to assess student learning.

Frequently Asked Questions

How did you define what a reading strategy is, and how did you choose which ones to use in the handbook?

In the *Reader's Handbook,* a **strategy** is defined as having a broad application across different genres. A strategy can serve a number of purposes. For example, you can *outline* or *find cause and effect* with fiction or nonfiction, a textbook, or a test. But some skills, such as *drawing conclusions* or *comparing and contrasting,* are so fundamental that they underlie almost everything. That's why these skills are called **reading know-how.** The handbook also refers to **reading tools,** which are more specialized and have a specific use or purpose. The Reader's Almanac lists 38 key reading tools used throughout the handbook. A Cause-Effect Organizer, for example, is used with nonfiction texts; Story Strings work specifically with fiction; Double-entry Journals work well for poetry. These distinctions between strategies, know-how, and tools are an attempt to use terms consistently in the absence of any consensus and an attempt to create a set of terms teachers can use within a school to create a shared, common language.

How did you decide on these specific steps of the reading process, and why are they in the order they are?

Reading is almost infinitely complex. It—like writing—hardly follows any single process or, for that matter, works in any single direction. But students need specifics on what to do. They need a good model, and they need to develop good habits. So, rather than presenting reading in all its complex splendor, the handbook organizes reading around an easy-to-remember process, explaining what students need to do Before, During, and After Reading. It breaks down the process into brief, easy steps. As with the writing process, students may sometimes skip a step, go backward occasionally, or spend a long time on one of the steps. That's OK. The reading process will help students make the decisions they need in order to be effective readers.

What kind of students is the handbook for?

The *Reader's Handbook* is for all students. Different students will take away different things from the handbook. Good readers will refine the strategies they use and learn some new reading tools, and perhaps they will learn even more about how different kinds of texts are organized. Average readers will add to the reading strategies and tools they use, and they'll develop a stronger understanding of the reading process. In addition, students who struggle will acquire some good strategies, tools, and understanding of the reading process.

Where should I begin as a teacher?

For help in teaching the handbook, start with the *Teacher's Guide* and *Overhead Transparencies*. To develop a curriculum or daily lesson plans, start with the *Lesson Plan Book* for your grade. To see if students can apply the strategies, use the *Student Applications Book* for your grade.

What is the difference between the *Lesson Plan Book* and *Teacher's Guide*?

The *Teacher's Guide* guides teachers through the chapters and lessons in the handbook in the order that they are presented. It points out what to emphasize in each chapter or lesson and provides more background. The *Lesson Plan Book* breaks the handbook into "class-period-size" chunks of 30 minutes, helping teachers see, for example, how to divide an 18-page lesson on the short story over one or two weeks.

You do not need to juggle both books at the same time. Use the *Teacher's Guide* if you are using the handbook as a resource. Use the *Lesson Plan Book* if you are using the handbook to teach a reading curriculum. The *Lesson Plan Book* lays out a complete reading curriculum for each year, and it shows ways to design a reading curriculum of your own. Consult, too, the Lesson Plan Library at the website (www.greatsource.com/rehand) for additional lesson plans.

How can I adapt the *Reader's Handbook* program to meet the individual needs of my students?

To succeed as readers, students need to work with appropriate-level materials. Materials that are too hard, albeit on grade level, will only frustrate struggling readers and deepen their aversion to trying again. To avoid this problem, the *Reader's Handbook* program has been organized so that teachers can accommodate students' varying reading levels.

The basic idea is simple. If the handbook seems too hard for your students, focus on one strategy and one or two readings tools and apply them to material that students are able to read easily. If the handbook seems too easy for your students, ask them to apply the reading strategies and tools to more sophisticated texts. See pages 18–19 of this book to learn how to individualize the *Reader's Handbook* to meet your students' needs.

For more Frequently Asked Questions, see the website at www.greatsource.com/rehand.

Reading Curriculum

Each *Lesson Plan Book* suggests a reading curriculum for teachers to implement in their classrooms. This curriculum was designed for a 36-week school year, and it shows what a teacher can reasonably cover in a single year. For convenience, the *Lesson Plan Book* organizes lesson plans into two-week segments, so you can see at a glance all of the daily lessons and resources for a genre.

To customize a curriculum for your students, see pages 14–17.

Grade 9 Curriculum

Week	Unit
1	Introduction
2	The Reading Process
3	Reading Know-how
4	Reading Paragraphs
5	Reading History
6	Reading Science
7	Reading Math
8	Elements of Textbooks
9	Reading a Personal Essay
10	Reading a Memoir
11	Reading an Editorial
12	Focus on Speeches
13	Elements of Nonfiction
14	Reading a Short Story
15	Focus on Plot
16	Focus on Setting
17	Focus on Characters
18	Reading a Novel

Week	Unit
19	Focus on Theme
20	Elements of Fiction
21	Elements of Poetry
22	Reading a Poem
23	Focus on Meaning, Sound, and Structure
24	Reading a Play
25	Focus on Language and Theme
26	Focus on Shakespeare
27	Reading a Website
28	Reading a Graphic
29	Reading for the Everyday World
30	Reading Tests and Test Questions
31	Focus on Writing Tests
32	Focus on History and Standardized Tests
33	Focus on Math Tests
34	Improving Vocabulary
35	The Reader's Almanac
36	The Reader's Almanac

Grade 10 Curriculum

Grade 11 Curriculum

Week	Unit
1	Reading Process/ Reading Know-how
2	Improving Vocabulary
3	Doing Research
4	Reading History
5	Focus on Foreign Language
6	Reading Math
7	Focus on Word Problems
8	Elements of Textbooks
9	Reading a Personal Essay
10	Reading an Editorial
11	Focus on Persuasive Writing
12	Focus on Speeches
13	Reading a Short Story
14	Focus on Theme
15	Focus on Comparing and Contrasting
16	Elements of Fiction
17	Reading a Novel
18	Reading a Novel

Week	Unit
19	Reading a Poem
20	Focus on Sound and Structure
21	Focus on Meaning
22	Focus on Meaning
23	Elements of Poetry
24	Elements of Poetry
25	Reading a Play
26	Focus on Theme
27	Focus on Shakespeare
28	Elements of the Internet
29	Reading a Website
30	Reading a Graphic
31	Elements of Graphics
32	Focus on Reading Instructions
33	Reading Tests and Test Questions
34	Focus on English Tests
35	Strategy Handbook
36	Reading Tools

Grade 12 Curriculum

Build Your Own Curriculum

The lesson plans in the *Lesson Plan Book* are adaptable to fit any curriculum. You can pick and choose lessons to teach with a specific emphasis. You can also use lesson plans from other grade levels, which are available from the website (www.greatsource.com/rehand). See the examples below and on the next page for suggestions to design your own curriculum.

Example

Use the year-long Curriculum Plan to map out which chapters to teach in each quarter. The example below shows a model that emphasizes teaching reading across the curriculum.

Reading Across the Curriculum Focus

Quarter 1	Quarter 2
Reading Process Reading Know-how Reading Textbooks	Reading Textbooks Reading Nonfiction
Quarter 3	**Quarter 4**
Reading Fiction Reading Poetry Reading Graphics	Reading Drama Reading on the Internet Reading for Tests Improving Vocabulary

Quarter 1 Plan

Week 1 Process	Reading
Week 2 Know-how	Reading
Week 3 Know-how	Reading
Week 4 Elements of Textbooks	
Week 5 History	Reading
Week 6 History	Reading

Once a Curriculum Plan is set for the year, create a Quarter Plan to help you focus on which lessons to teach week by week during each quarter.

Other Year-long Curriculum Plan Examples

Vocabulary and Language Focus

Quarter 1	Quarter 2
Reading Process Reading Know-how Improving Vocabulary Reading Textbooks	Reading Fiction Reading Poetry Reading Nonfiction Reading for Tests

Quarter 3	Quarter 4
Reading Textbooks Reading Nonfiction Reading Poetry Improving Vocabulary	Reading Graphics Reading Drama Improving Vocabulary Reading for Tests

Literature Focus

Quarter 1	Quarter 2
Reading Process Reading Know-how Improving Vocabulary Reading Fiction	Reading Fiction Reading Poetry Improving Vocabulary Reading for Tests

Quarter 3	Quarter 4
Reading Textbooks Reading Nonfiction Reading Drama Reading Poetry	Reading Nonfiction Reading Graphics Reading on the Internet Reading for Tests

Test-Success Focus

Quarter 1	Quarter 2
Reading Process Reading Know-how Improving Vocabulary Reading for Tests	Reading Textbooks Reading Graphics Reading Nonfiction Reading for Tests

Quarter 3	Quarter 4
Reading Fiction Reading Poetry Improving Vocabulary Reading for Tests	Reading Drama Reading on the Internet Reading Textbooks Reading for Tests

Build Your Own Curriculum

CURRICULUM:_____

1st Quarter	2nd Quarter

3rd Quarter	4th Quarter

Name:______________________________

Build Your Own Curriculum

QUARTER:______________________________

Week 1 ______________________________

Week 2 ______________________________

Week 3 ______________________________

Week 4 ______________________________

Week 5 ______________________________

Week 6 ______________________________

Week 7 ______________________________

Week 8 ______________________________

Week 9 ______________________________

Meeting Students' Individual Needs

The Reader's Handbook *program is organized so that teachers can accommodate students' varying reading levels. The handbook itself is written to the ninth through twelfth grade level, but that readability does not limit the usefulness of the handbook for students who are very highly developed in reading or for students who are struggling.*

For Highly Developed Readers

Even strong readers will benefit from the *Reader's Handbook*. The reading strategies and tools explained in the handbook are rarely in common usage even with the very best readers. The desire to use "harder" or "more sophisticated" materials should extend more to the reading materials to which students are applying the handbook's strategies and tools. The world of students' reading is what is more sophisticated, not necessarily their command of reading strategies and tools.

Here are some ideas to try with your most highly developed readers:

1. Independent Application
Ask students to apply the strategy and tools in a specific lesson to their own materials. For example, after teaching Reading History, ask students to apply the strategy of note-taking and the note-taking tools to a chapter in their own history text.

2. Buddy Learning
Ask students to "teach" the lesson to other students in small groups. Use the highly developed readers to "tutor" students who need more help. The experience of explaining the strategy and reading tools to other readers will reinforce the ideas, as well as help the students who are being tutored.

3. Reading Exercises
To stretch students to the topmost level of their learning zone and challenge them, create reading exercises using sophisticated materials that are clearly challenging for them to read. By experiencing a difficult text and having to rely on the strategies and tools, students will be challenged to use more than just one or two reading strategies. As a teacher, you need to monitor students' frustration levels so that they do not become discouraged. The point of the exercises is to give students' command of reading strategies and tools a test, not to break their spirit.

For Struggling Readers

Struggling readers can also benefit greatly from the *Reader's Handbook*. Most students who struggle as readers have few reading strategies and tools to call upon, and their grasp of the reading process is probably somewhat vague, if they even see it as a process at all.

As a teacher, try not to focus on having students "cover" the material. Focus instead on helping students develop a stronger reading process and in becoming adept with **one reading strategy** and **two or three reading tools**. The desire to use "easier" materials with struggling readers should focus on the reading materials to which students are applying the handbook's strategies and tools.

Here are some ideas to try with struggling readers:

1. Easier Texts

Ask students to apply the strategy and tools in a specific lesson to texts that are very easy for them. Help students find a text that is appropriate to their reading level. Then help them apply the reading process, a reading strategy, and a reading tool to it. Success with an easy text will show students how to apply these strategies to more challenging materials.

Limit your objectives for these students to a few main things:

■ Focus on one (or perhaps two) reading strategies at most.

■ Try out 3–5 reading tools and help struggling readers master one or two of them so that they are comfortable using them on materials that are easy for them to read.

■ Help students apply the single strategy and reading tool to their own textbooks.

2. Guided Reading of the Handbook

■ Before beginning a lesson, work with students to preview the material in the handbook. Have students predict what they think the chapter or lesson will be about. Then explain that you will use a reading process. Reading starts *before* the eyes begin moving. What will a lesson called "Focus on Word Problems" be about?

■ Preferably you will work with a small group of students, leading them through the lesson. Focus on the basic parts of the reading process, building background for students at each step of the lesson.

■ Stress to students the importance of rereading. After they finish reading the first time, help students see that they don't have to "know it all." That is the time to go back and "fix up" the holes in their understanding, using another strategy or tool.

3. Paired Reading and Questioning

By pairing students together, you can help struggling readers by giving them a "buddy" to help guide them through a lesson. Then, ask students to ask each other questions on each page.

Reading Strategies Overview

Handbook Lesson	Selection	Reading Strategy	Rereading Strategy
Reading History	"The Rise of Islam"	Note-taking	Using Graphic Organizers
Reading Science	"Biology in Your World"	Outlining	Note-taking
Reading Math	"Numbers and Number Operations"	Visualizing and Thinking Aloud	Note-taking
Reading a Personal Essay	"The Indian Dog" by N. Scott Momaday	Outlining	Questioning the Author
Reading an Editorial	"College Sports Myth Versus Math"	Questioning the Author	Synthesizing
Reading a News Story	"Violent Images May Alter Kids' Brain Activity"	Reading Critically	Summarizing
Reading a Biography	*Rickey & Robinson* by John C. Chalberg	Looking for Cause and Effect	Outlining
Reading a Memoir	*Out of Africa* by Isak Dinesen	Synthesizing	Visualizing and Thinking Aloud
Reading a Short Story	"Powder" by Tobias Wolff	Synthesizing	Close Reading
Reading a Novel	*All Quiet on the Western Front* by Erich Maria Remarque	Using Graphic Organizers	Synthesizing
Reading a Poem	"Sonnet 43" by Elizabeth Barrett Browning	Close Reading	Paraphrasing
Reading a Play	*The Miracle Worker* by William Gibson	Summarizing	Visualizing and Thinking Aloud
Reading a Website	Google search engine and "National Gallery of Art" site	Reading Critically	Skimming
Reading a Graphic	"Digital Kids"	Paraphrasing	Reading Critically
Reading a Driver's Handbook	from *Rules of the Road*	Skimming	Visualizing and Thinking Aloud
Reading Tests	"The Laugher" by Heinrich Böll	Skimming	Visualizing and Thinking Aloud

Focus Lesson	Selection	Reading Strategy /Tools
Focus on Foreign Language	"Vocabulario y gramática"	Note-taking
Focus on Science Concepts	"The Scientific Process"	Outlining
Focus on Study Questions	Sample Study Questions	Visualizing and Thinking Aloud
Focus on Word Problems	Sample Problem	Visualizing and Thinking Aloud
Focus on Persuasive Writing	"Appearances Are Destructive"	Reading Critically
Focus on Speeches	"Blood, Toil, Tears, and Sweat" by Winston Churchill	Reading Critically
Focus on Plot	from "Blues Ain't No Mockinbird" by Toni Cade Bambara	Using Graphic Organizers
Focus on Setting	from *Cry, the Beloved Country* by Alan Paton	Close Reading
Focus on Characters	from "The Necklace" by Guy de Maupassant	Using Graphic Organizers
Focus on Theme	*Jasmine* by Bharati Mukherjee	Using Graphic Organizers
Focus on Dialogue	from "Blues Ain't No Mockinbird"	Close Reading
Focus on Comparing and Contrasting	*David Copperfield* and *Great Expectations* by Charles Dickens	Using Graphic Organizers
Focus on Language	"Identity" by Julio Noboa Polanco	Close Reading
Focus on Meaning	"Ex-Basketball Player" by John Updike	Close Reading
Focus on Sound and Structure	"Suicide in the Trenches" by Siegfried Sassoon	Close Reading
Focus on Language	from *The Miracle Worker* by William Gibson	Inference Chart
Focus on Theme	from *The Miracle Worker*	Topic and Theme Organizer
Focus on Shakespeare	from *Romeo and Juliet* by William Shakespeare	Using Graphic Organizers
Focus on Reading Instructions	Cell Phone Instructions DVD Player Instructions	Close Reading
Focus on Reading for Work	Memo on Workplace Safety Job Description Work Schedule	Skimming
Focus on English Tests	*A Tale of Two Cities* by Charles Dickens	Skimming
Focus on Writing Tests	Sample Writing Test	Main Idea Organizer
Focus on Standardized Tests	Sample Questions	Think Aloud
Focus on History Tests	Sample History Test	Think Aloud
Focus on Math Tests	Sample Math Test	Visualizing and Thinking Aloud
Focus on Science Tests	Sample Science Test	Visualizing and Thinking Aloud

Guide to the *Reader's Handbook*

Reading Lessons

These lessons show students how to follow a step-by-step reading process to read different kinds of materials—from textbooks and websites to novels and poems.

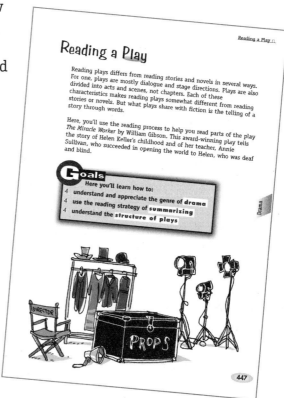

Each reading lesson includes several key features:

- ■ a list of **goals** that tell what the lesson is about
- ■ a **preview checklist** that tells what to look for in a particular type of reading
- ■ one **reading** and another **rereading strategy** to help students find the information they want
- ■ several **reading tools** to help students keep track of information
- ■ information on **how the text is organized**
- ■ a **summing up** box that highlights what students should remember

Focus Lessons

Focus lessons take a closer look at one type of reading or specific element, such as theme, setting, essay tests, and so on. They are shorter lessons that zero in on a single subject. A combination of reading tools, reading strategies, and tips is suggested to help students better understand the subject.

Elements Lessons

Elements lessons explain key terms related to the genre. Each lesson starts off with an **example,** so students see how the term is used. Next, students read a **description** about the term in the example. The lesson ends with a clear **definition**.

Reader's Almanac

The Reader's Almanac is a reference guide.

The **Strategy Handbook** describes in detail each of the 12 reading strategies.

Doing Research provides an overview of how to find useful material, keep track of information, and document sources.

The **Reading Tools** section describes and gives examples of the 38 reading tools.

Word Parts gives a list of prefixes, suffixes, and roots.

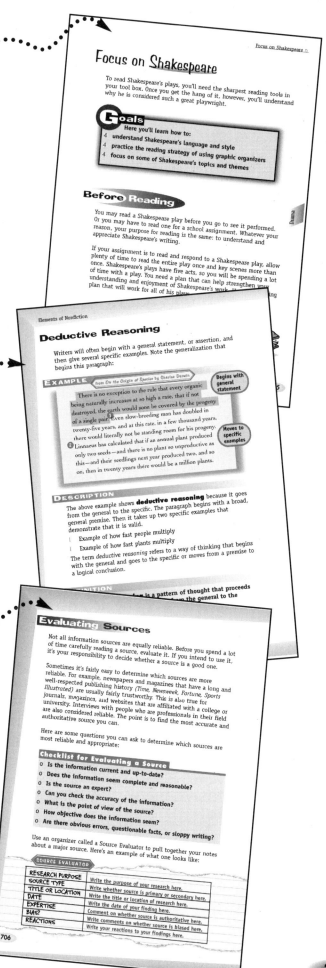

Correlations

Overview

The *Reader's Handbook* is a multifaceted guide to reading, and it easily supplements several other Great Source reading and writing products. Use the correlation charts that follow to integrate lessons with other Great Source materials.

1. *Daybooks of Critical Reading and Writing,* Grade 10

Like the *Reader's Handbook*, the *Daybooks* show students how to become active readers. The *Daybooks* complement the *Reader's Handbook* by offering further opportunities to practice using reading strategies and tools, the reading process, and reading know-how. The *Daybooks* have been correlated to the *Reader's Handbook* through the genre of the selections. In other words, nonfiction selections from the *Daybooks* are suggested for the Reading Nonfiction chapter in the handbook; poetry selections with Reading Poetry, and so on.

Reader's Handbook Chapter	*Daybook,* Grade 10	Pages
II. The Reading Process	"Mid-Term Break"	13–14
III. Reading Know-how	"Digging"	10
	"Blackberry-Picking"	11–12
	Quotes About Seamus Haney	18–20
IV. Reading Textbooks	from *Voices from Vietnam*	66–69
V. Reading Nonfiction	"The Nature of Symbolic Language"	25
	"A Name Is Sometimes An Ancestor Saying HI, I'm With You"	46–47
	from *Blue Highways: A Journey Into America*	54
	"The Marginal World"	55–57
	"Freedom and Wilderness"	58–60
	from *Blue Highways: A Journey Into America*	63–64
	from *When Heaven and Earth Changed Places*	70–73
	from *A Natural History of the Senses*	85–86
	from *Let Us Now Praise Famous Men*	92–94**
	from *Serve It Forth*	95–97
	"Bread"	98–102
	from "How It Feels To Be Colored Me"	204–206, 217–218
	"How God Made Butterflies" from *Mules and Men*	207–208, 217–218
VI. Reading Fiction	"The Man to Send Rain Clouds"	27–29
	"December 2001: The Green Morning"	30–34

2. *Reading and Writing Sourcebooks, Grade 10*

One way the *Reader's Handbook* can be used is to help struggling readers. The *Sourcebooks* focus on struggling readers, teach a reading process and reading tools, and encourage students to become active readers. In these three ways, the *Sourcebooks* complement the *Reader's Handbook*. To facilitate using both programs, each *Sourcebook* selection has been correlated to an appropriate chapter in the *Reader's Handbook*.

3. *Writers INC*

The main goal of the *Reader's Handbook* is to teach all students how to become better readers. *Writers INC* directly complements the handbook through its teaching of a writing process and how types of writing are organized. To teach both programs side by side, the correlation below shows which parts of *Writers INC* best complement individual chapters in the *Reader's Handbook*.

Reader's Handbook Chapter	Correlation	*Writers INC*
I. Introduction	understanding writing	1–2
II. The Reading Process	writing process	3–20
III. Reading Know-how	writing paragraphs	95–104
IV. Reading Textbooks	note-taking	394–395
V. Reading Nonfiction	essays	105–123
VI. Reading Fiction	novels	238,
	stories	170–172
VII. Reading Poetry	writing a poem	179–184
VIII. Reading Drama	writing a play	174–177
IX. Reading on the Internet	using the Internet	331–336
X. Reading Graphics	using graphs	352–353
XI. Reading for the Everyday World	workplace writing	296–321
XII. Reading for Tests	test-taking skills	405–419
XIII. Improving Vocabulary	improving vocabulary	367–381

The Challenge of High School Readers

by Jim Burke

It has never been easier *not* to read; yet the same set of skills remains essential to students' success in the world. Access to online "study guides" and the pretense that skimming for the bold words equals understanding—these and other such modern conveniences highlight the challenges of high school readers. The students themselves are challenged by the growing array and sophistication of texts, texts which include colors and symbols alongside words and images. Teachers, too, are challenged by the needs of readers at all levels as students struggle to read those texts most challenging to them at the levels most appropriate to their current skill level.

To meet these challenges and those that await our students in the adult world, students must develop the craft of reading (Scholes, 2001). According to Scholes, "As with any craft, reading depends on the use of certain tools, handled with skill" (2001). Craft, as Scholes goes on to emphasize, can be taught because it is based on skills that can be studied and taught. The *Reader's Handbook* shows students how to read the texts they encounter in all their classes; it demystifies the process of reading, thereby developing the student's "textual intelligence" (Burke, 2001), even as it adds a range of tools to the student's intellectual toolbelt (Schoenbach, et al., 1999).

Reading the table of contents of the *Reader's Handbook* is like walking through a huge mall or a megastore. Both students and teachers alike confront the fact that ours is a textual world. You don't just read the newspaper; instead, you read editorials, ads, comics, maps, graphs, and infographics. All of them try to accomplish something different, using different conventions and demanding the reader use different "tools" to make sense of the text. The same goes for content area literacy. Textbooks are made up of many different demanding types of texts. For example, the reader must try to understand the visual explanation of a map within the context of a chapter on World War II.

High school teachers have long felt that students arrive—or should—having learned how to read. Reading now means reading to learn about content. The challenge of high school readers, especially when students come from such diverse backgrounds and enter the class with such different needs, is that they mostly do know "how to read" but rarely know how to read the different types of texts they study or those they will encounter in newspapers, contracts, college classes, or workplaces. Just as batting coaches teach players how to "read the pitcher," teachers today must teach students how to read those texts central to their discipline. The science teacher must not only help students master the multicolored, crowded pages of the six-pound textbook but must also teach them how to read the different tests and the tables, charts, articles, experiments, and results common to any lively science class. The same goes for English teachers and social science teachers, not to mention the math teachers who find their own textbooks increasingly weighed down by words and concepts which challenge their students.

The *Reader's Handbook* is *not* written specifically for students with reading difficulties. Think of it as an anthology of practices, a collection of strategies that will benefit all students at all levels. It offers, to return to the toolbelt analogy, a set of tools designed to make all students more strategic readers. It does this by introducing them to the reading process and then giving them a range of strategies they can employ at different stages of that process. These different strategies and those tools found in the Reader's Almanac of the *Reader's Handbook* are just as useful to the advanced reader as they are to the struggling reader. While the less skilled reader learns to use the reading process to comprehend the basic action of the story or the main idea of the essay, the *Reader's Handbook* expands the developing and sophisticated readers' abilities to read for meaning and style, showing them how the author organizes ideas and uses words to create a certain tone or develop a theme.

The challenge of high school readers is sometimes exacerbated by the challenges schools face. Lack of time needed for teachers to collaborate and plan means students encounter a maze of methods and general absence of coherent, schoolwide strategies. The *Reader's Handbook* provides a set of clearly defined, classroom-tested techniques—applied to the very texts most commonly taught in high schools—that will improve students' abilities to read those texts as much as it will strengthen a teacher's own ability to teach them. It is our hope that the *Reader's Handbook* will create a schoolwide vocabulary of techniques. Thus, when the teacher begins a new text, all the students will know they need to begin by setting a purpose, previewing, "making connections" as they read, and so on. When students get stuck—whether reading Shakespeare, a difficult test, or a textbook—they and their teachers will be able to refer to the handbook and ask which strategy will be most effective in this situation.

Let's face it, with the demands of high school these days—the pace, the quantity of work, the increased standards and high expectations—students can easily feel challenged, even afraid. They quickly lose confidence as they begin taking those large history exams and reading that science book written for more advanced readers. When they receive their first major novel in high school, they lose motivation to read it because they worry they cannot keep up, that they will not understand it, that they cannot understand it. The *Reader's Handbook* demystifies the reading process, turning reading into a craft instead of an art. People can learn, even master a craft, because it can be taught. Following the same steps in the process in each chapter, students learn by first watching the *Reader's Handbook* model, and then applying the same techniques. While the more skilled reader benefits from the book's demonstrations, learning to recognize the more subtle elements of, for example, a poem or a Shakespearean play, developing readers learn that by following the steps in the process they *can* read a poem, they *can* understand Shakespeare. In subsequent years, as readers' capacities develop, the handbook supports their progress by showing them how to read those more challenging aspects of the texts.

This distinction between struggling and sophisticated readers merits further discussion as the *Reader's Handbook* is written for them both. Students in advanced or honors classes — even AP (Advanced Placement) classes—too often pretend they understand what they read (Tovani, 2000). They become reliant on various study aids to give them the insights they are incapable of arriving at on their own. Such a "strategy" is a bit like having someone else do your exercise for you. It catches up with these advanced students who do not "learn to fish" on their own. They might get out of high school, even graduate with good grades, but when they arrive at college, they suddenly find themselves unprepared and ill-equipped to read the literature and textbooks their professors assign and expect them to read independently. While writing the *Reader's Handbook*, I taught both struggling readers (a program called ACCESS, which stands for Academic Success) and freshman honors English. I routinely tried out what I wrote with both groups, making sure it was not only readable but useful to both groups of students. Honors students can read and comprehend the basic plot of a short story like Tobias Wolff's "Powder" (see page 270), but they miss the multiple meanings, the connotative meanings of words, the devices Wolff uses to create tension between the father and son. The *Reader's Handbook* develops their critical reading abilities, turning their intuitive or natural reading talents into a set of conscious, effective decisions and skills that allow them to read a range of increasingly sophisticated texts common to advanced students.

The handbook supports students in several different ways. Foremost, it provides a powerful way to teach specific skills needed to read the texts teachers need to teach and students must know how to read. Second, it gives students a readily available guide to help them troubleshoot their own reading when not in class. Just as a computer user reaches for the manual to resolve some confusion, or the mechanic consults a manual to troubleshoot some problem encountered while repairing a car, so, too, a student can refer to the *Reader's Handbook* while preparing for a big exam or tackling a tough assignment. Here, for example, students can find useful strategies designed to make them more effective, intelligent readers of different types of tests. Or, should they find themselves struggling to read Shakespeare, students can go to the "Focus on Shakespeare" lesson and get tips they need to be successful.

The world of texts has changed in ways that not even Shakespeare himself could have anticipated. If Shakespeare's plays were the only challenge to high school students today, a book like the *Reader's Handbook* would not be necessary. Yet the Internet, the proliferation of tests, the growing complexity of many textbooks, and the developmental needs of today's students make this book essential reading. Students rarely form relationships with books, for they too often see school books as obstacles to their success instead of guides that will insure their success. Students new to the United States quickly learn that the dictionary is their key to the world of language. The *Reader's Handbook* offers a similar key, one that not only opens the world of different texts but the world beyond high school and even college, the world for which these four years is but a preparation.

References

Burke, J. (2001) *Illuminating Texts: How to Teach Students to Read the World*. Portsmouth, NH: Heinemann.

Scholes, (2001). *The Crafty Reader*. New Haven, CT: Yale University Press.

Schoenbach, R., Greenleaf, C., Cziko, C., & Huwritz, L. (1999) *Reading for Understanding*. San Francisco, CA: Joseey-Bass.

Tovani, C. & Keene, E. O. (2000). *I Read It, but I Don't Get It: Comprehension Strategies for Adolescent Readers*. Portland, ME: Stenhouse Pub.

Reader's Handbook, Grades 9-12, Research Base

by April D. Nauman, Ph.D.

It is commonly believed that once students reach high school, they can or should be able to read their assignments without additional help. Recently, however, many educators and researchers have challenged this assumption. Vacca (1998) points out that "literacy use becomes increasingly more complex and demanding" in adolescence (p. 606). High school students must read, comprehend, and remember information in a variety of high-level content area textbooks, which are packed with new concepts and vocabulary. In addition, high school students are expected to read and analyze canonized adult literature, much of which contains unfamiliar language and complex structures, characters, and themes. These expectations occur at a time when students' motivation to read tends to decline (Bintz, 1997; McKenna, Kear, & Ellsworth, 1996). For all these reasons, many educators have advocated for systematic literacy instruction at the high school level (Avery & Avery, 1996; Bintz, 1997; Gauthier & Smith, 1993; International Reading Association, 1999; Vacca, 1998; Vacca & Vacca, 2002). The *Reader's Handbook* for grades 9–12 provides teachers with a tool for such instruction.

The *Reader's Handbook* is based in current research on reading. Such research has established that good reading is a strategic process: successful readers use a variety of strategies to construct the meaning of the text (Pearson, Roehler, Dole, & Duffy, 1992). These strategies include connecting what is read to prior knowledge, monitoring understanding, distinguishing important from less important information, self-questioning, and making inferences during and after reading. Less successful readers often lack knowledge of or control over such strategies, not quite understanding when or how to use them to learn from text (Vacca & Vacca, 2002). Fortunately, research also shows that less capable readers can be taught these strategies, resulting in improved reading comprehension (e.g., Pressley, 2000).

The *Reader's Handbook* for grades 9–12 is a student resource full of reading and study strategies endorsed by researchers, teacher educators, and classroom teachers. Some of these strategies have been used successfully for years; others are new, ground-breaking approaches that enhance critical reading and student engagement in text. The strategies are applied to a wide range of genres, from textbooks to popular media to literature. Because it can be used without continuous teacher guidance, the *Reader's Handbook* promotes student independence and responsibility for gaining control of the reading and study strategies needed to succeed academically.

Avery, C.W., & Avery, B.F. (1996). On the road to school reform: Mapping a route into secondary reading programs. *Journal of Adolescent and Adult Literacy,* 40, 214-217.

Bintz, W.P. (1997). Exploring reading nightmares of middle and secondary school teachers. *Journal of Adolescent and Adult Literacy,* 41, 12-24.

Gauthier, M.G., & Smith, E.L. (1993). Whole school supplemental reading program. *Journal of Reading,* 37, 135-139.

International Reading Association (1999). Adolescent literacy comes of age. *Reading Today,* 17(1), 1, 22.
McKenna, M.C., Kear, D.J., & Ellsworth, R.A. (1995). Children's attitudes toward reading: A national survey. *Research Reading Quarterly,* 30, 934-955.

Pearson, P. D., Roehler, L. R., Dole, J. A., & Duffy, G. G. (1992). Developing expertise in reading comprehension. In S. J. Samuels and A. E. Farstrup (Eds.), *What research has to say about reading instruction*. Newark, DE: International Reading Association.

Pressley, M. (2000). Comprehension instruction in elementary school: A quarter-century of research progress. In B. M. Taylor, F. F. Graves, and P. van den Broek (Eds.), *Reading for meaning: Fostering comprehension in the middle grades*. Newark, DE: International Reading Association.

Vacca, R.T. (1998). Let's not marginalize adolescent literacy. *Journal of Adolescent and Adult Literacy*, 41, 604-609.

Vacca, R. T., & Vacca, J. L. (2002). *Content area reading: Literacy and learning across the curriculum* (7th ed.). Boston: Allyn & Bacon.

Introduction

Chapter 1 introduces students to the reading process, emphasizing what reading is and why it's important. The chapter defines reading in ways that high school students may not have thought about before: Reading is a set of habits and abilities, reading is thinking, and reading is power. Successful reading also requires tools, which are provided in the *Reader's Handbook*.

The chapter also explains the purposes for reading, including academic, personal, for the workplace, and to function in society. High school students need to understand that reading is not just something adults make them do, but an essential life skill they will need when they become adults themselves (Vacca & Vacca, 2002).

In a special section on "Reading as a Process," the *Reader's Handbook* clearly elucidates what effective readers do before, during, and after reading. These characteristics of effective reading are based in current reading research. For example, effective readers establish a purpose and make predictions before reading (Heilman, Blair, & Rupley, 2002; Pearson, Roehler, Dole, & Duffy, 1992). During reading, effective readers check their understanding and make connections between the text and their own experiences (Ruddell & Rudell, 1994; Wilhelm, 1997). After reading, effective readers re-check their understanding, ask themselves if they met their initial reading purposes, and review the text (Anderson and Armbruster, 1984; Heilman, et al., 2002).

Finally, to help students fully grasp the concept of reading as a process, Chapter 1 likens it to the writing process. The writing process approach is currently one of the most common ways of teaching writing in high schools. Popularized by Donald Graves (1991, 1994), Lucy Calkins (1994), and others (e.g., Hillocks, 1987), this approach is endorsed by virtually all major teacher educators and researchers (e.g., Cooper, 2000). The writing process approach enables students to gain control of the complex task of writing by identifying the stages that expert writers go through while working. The complex task of reading can be simplified in much the same way.

Anderson, T. H., & Armbruster, B. B. (1984). Studying. In P. D. Pearson, R. Barr, M. L. Kamil, & P. Mosenthal (Eds.), *Handbook of reading research* (pp. 657-679). New York: Longman.

Calkins, L. M. (1994). *The art of teaching writing*. Portsmouth, NH: Heinemann.

Cooper, J. D. (2000). *Literacy: Helping children construct meaning* (4th ed.). Boston: Houghton Mifflin.

Graves, D. H. (1991). *Build a literate classroom.* Portsmouth, NH: Heinemann.

Graves, D. H. (1994). *A fresh look at writing.* Portsmouth, NH: Heinemann.

Heilman, A. W., Blair, T. R., & Rupley, W. H. (2002). *Principles and practices of teaching reading* (10th ed.). Upper Saddle River, NJ: Merrill Prentice Hall.

Hillocks, G., Jr. (1987). Synthesis of research on teaching writing. *Educational Leadership, 44,* 71-82.

Pearson, P. D., Roehler, L. R., Dole, J. A., & Duffy, G. G. (1992). Developing expertise in reading comprehension. In S. J. Samuels and A. E. Farstrup (Eds.), *What research has to say about reading instruction.* Newark, DE: International Reading Association.

Ruddell, R. B., & Ruddell, M. R. (1994). Language acquisition and literacy process. In R. B. Ruddell, M. R. Ruddell, & H. Singer (Eds.), *Theoretical models and processes of reading* (4th ed., pp. 448-468). Newark, DE: International Reading Association.

Wilhelm, J. (1997). *"You gotta BE the book": Teaching engaged and reflective reading with adolescents.* New York: Teachers College Press.

Vacca, R. T., & Vacca, J. L. (2002). *Content area reading: Literacy and learning across the curriculum* (7th ed.). Boston: Allyn & Bacon.

The Reading Process

In Chapter 2 of the *Reader's Handbook,* the reading process is explained step by step. Before reading, students are to set a purpose, preview, and plan. During reading, students read with a purpose and connect with the text. After reading, students pause and reflect, reread, and remember.

Research shows that purpose setting and previewing a text before reading can help less capable readers become skilled, strategic readers (Heilman, Blair, & Rupley, 2002; Paris, Lipson, & Wilson, 1994). Purpose setting, previewing, and planning enable students to better apply reading strategies during and after reading (Heilman, et al., 2002). For example, the student who determines his or her purpose before reading can then use that purpose to identify and focus on the most important information in the text.

Connecting with text during reading, promotes student engagement with the material. Successful adolescent readers connect with or relate to texts in a variety of ways, whereas less capable readers do not (Wilhelm, 1997). Making connections between the text and personal experiences, other texts, and other subjects is the route to activating prior knowledge, and comprehension relies on linking what is read to what is already known (Ruddell & Ruddell, 1994.)

After reading, students are to pause and reflect, reread, and remember. Educators and researchers have long recognized the need for students to look back at the text to reread or review what they did not understand during reading (Heilman, Blair, & Rupley, 2002). Rereading is especially important for learning from content area textbooks (Anderson & Armbruster, 1984) and for struggling readers (Vacca & Vacca, 2002). The pause-and-reflect step of the after-reading process is integral to comprehension and strategic reading, as students must consider whether they met their purpose for reading. Students also identify parts of the text that were confusing and need to be reread.

Anderson, T. H., & Armbruster, B. B. (1984). Studying. In P. D. Pearson, R. Barr, M. L. Kamil, & P. Mosenthal (Eds.), *Handbook of reading research* (pp. 657-679). New York: Longman.

Heilman, A. W., Blair, T. R., & Rupley, W. H. (2002). *Principles and practices of teaching reading* (10th ed.). Upper Saddle River, NJ: Merrill Prentice Hall.

Paris, S. G., Lipson, M. Y., & Wilson, K. K. (1994). Becoming a strategic reader. In R. B. Rudell, M. R. Ruddell, & H. Singer (Eds.), *Theoretical models and processes of reading* (4th ed., pp. 788-810). Newark, DE: International Reading Association.

Ruddell, R. B., & Ruddell, M. R. (1994). Language acquisition and literacy process. In R. B. Ruddell, M. R. Ruddell, & H. Singer (Eds.), *Theoretical models and processes of reading* (4th ed., pp. 448-468). Newark, DE: International Reading Association.

Vacca, R. T., & Vacca, J. L. (2002). *Content area reading: Literacy and learning across the curriculum* (7th ed.). Boston: Allyn & Bacon.

Wilhelm, J. (1997). *"You gotta BE the book": Teaching engaged and reflective reading with adolescents.* New York: Teachers College Press.

Reading Know-how

Chapter 3, "Reading Know-How," explains key skills that students need to construct meaning effectively while reading. Making inferences, reading actively, predicting, and asking questions are essential to comprehension (e.g., Cooper, 2000).

Research shows that readers must have inferential and reasoning skills to connect information in the text to relevant prior knowledge (van den Broek & Kremer, 2000). Prior knowledge alone is not enough; students must be able to infer—to use their prior knowledge to "fill in the gaps" in the text. Instruction in the process of inference enhances reading comprehension among high school students (e.g., Vacca & Vacca, 2002).

Making inferences is only one component of active reading. The handbook suggests six ways to read actively: marking up or highlighting the text, asking questions, clarifying, connecting to the reading, visualizing, and predicting. These are some important strategies used by expert readers (Pearson, Roehler, Dole, & Duffy, 1992). Making predictions during reading is especially important for adolescents, because it keeps them interested and engaged in increasingly difficult texts. Predicting is one of a set of strategies and activities recommended for adolescent students who struggle with reading (Dana, 1989). Questioning during reading also promotes engagement with the text and improves meaning construction (Davey & McBride, 1986; Singer & Donlan, 1982). Questioning and predicting while reading enable students to make essential connections to prior knowledge.

"Reading Know-how" also includes the important skill of identifying important information, or finding the main idea. Research shows that knowledge of text structure helps students identify important information in a reading (Dole, Duffy, Roehler, & Pearson, 1991). Almost all educators recognize the value of teaching text structure to improve comprehension and retention (e.g., Cooper, 2000). Accordingly, the *Reader's Handbook* defines and gives examples of different paragraph and text structures, which will help students develop an awareness of text patterns (Horowitz, 1985). This, in turn, will enhance their ability to identify important information and improve their comprehension.

Cooper, J. D. (2000). *Literacy: Helping children construct meaning* (4th ed.). Boston: Houghton Mifflin.

Dana, C. (1989). Strategy families for disabled readers. *Journal of Reading*, 33, 30-35.

Davey, B., & McBride, S. (1986). Effects of question generating training on reading comprehension. *Journal of Educational Psychology*, 78, 256-262.

Dole, J. A., Duffy, G. G., Roehler, L. R., & Pearson, P. D. (1991). Moving from the old to the new: Research on reading comprehension instruction. *Review of Educational Research*, 61, 239-264.

Horowitz, R. (1985). Text patterns. *Journal of Reading*, 28, 448-454.

Pearson, P. D., Roehler, L. R., Dole, J. A., & Duffy, G. G. (1992). Developing expertise in reading comprehension. In S. J. Samuels and A. E. Farstrup (Eds.), *What research has to say about reading instruction*. Newark, DE: International Reading Association.

Singer, H., & Donlan, D. (1982). Active comprehension: Problem-solving schema with question generation for comprehension of complex short stories. *Reading Research Quarterly*, 17, 166-186.

Vacca, R. T., & Vacca, J. L. (2002). *Content area reading: Literacy and learning across the curriculum* (7th ed.). Boston: Allyn & Bacon.

van den Broek, P., & Kremer, K. E. (2000). The mind in action: What it means to comprehend during reading. In B. M. Taylor, M. F. Graves, & P. van den Broek (Eds.), *Reading for meaning: Fostering comprehension in the middle grades* (pp. 1-31). New York: Teachers College Press.

Reading Textbooks

High school-level textbooks tend to be very challenging, containing difficult concepts and vocabulary. Chapter 4, "Reading Textbooks," provides important strategies for students to effectively learn from these books.

Research shows that most students' difficulty with textbooks results from a lack of knowledge about expository text structure (Cheek, Flippo, & Lindsey, 1997). Expository text structure varies more widely than narrative text structure (Cooper, 2000). A student's general reading ability does not necessarily indicate how well he or she will comprehend texts in the content areas (Leal & Moss, 1999). According to Heilman and colleagues (2002), learning from textbooks requires specific skills and strategies for reading in different subjects; study skills; and skills and strategies for collecting, analyzing, and evaluating data.

Note-taking is widely acknowledged as a valuable way to learn from textbooks (e.g., Vacca & Vacca, 2002). The handbook's "structured note" techniques, which require students to take notes using different graphic organizers, enable students to identify important ideas and organize the information (Smith & Tompkins, 1988). Structured note-taking techniques are more effective than simply jotting down isolated facts, because students must think about the text and decide what information and ideas are most important (Alvermann & Moore, 1991; Anderson & Armbruster, 1984).

Alvermann, D. E., & Moore, D. W. (1991). Secondary schools. In R. Barr, M. L. Kamil, P. B. Mosenthal, & P. D. Pearson (Eds.), *Handbook of reading research* (Vol. 2, pp. 951-983). New York: Longman.

Anderson, T. H., & Armbruster, B. B. (1984). Studying. In P. D. Pearson (Ed.), *Handbook of reading research* (pp. 657-679). New York: Longman.

Cheek, E. H., Flippo, R. F., & Lindsey, J. D. (1997). *Reading for success in elementary schools*. Dubuque, IA: Brown & Benchmark.

Cooper, J. D. (2000). *Literacy: Helping children construct meaning* (4th ed.). Boston: Houghton Mifflin.

Heilman, A. W., Blair, T. R., & Rupley, W. H. (2002). Principles and practices of teaching reading (10th ed.). Upper Saddle River, NJ: Merrill Prentice Hall.

Leal, D., & Moss, B. (1999). Encounters with information text: Perceptions and insights from four gifted readers. *Reading Horizons*, 40, 15-22.

Smith, P. L., & Tompkins, G. E. (1988). Structured notetaking: A new strategy for content area readers. *Journal of Reading*, 32, 46-53.

Vacca, R. T., & Vacca, J. L. (2002). *Content area reading: Literacy and learning across the curriculum* (7th ed.). Boston: Allyn & Bacon.

Reading Nonfiction

Chapter 5 presents strategies for understanding other nonfiction, such as essays, editorials, news stories, biographies, memoirs, and speeches. The strategies defined and illustrated include structured note-taking, summarizing, reading critically, and questioning the author."

Summarizing requires readers to reduce a text to its main ideas, which necessitates reflection on and interaction with the text. Readers who can summarize are able to differentiate important from less important information (Heilman, Blair, & Rupley, 2002). Summarizing is an important strategy for students at all grade levels and is especially recommended for struggling adolescent readers (Dana, 1989). Less capable readers can learn this strategy and improve their comprehension (Brown & Day, 1983).

Critical reading involves reflecting on what is being read, suspending judgment, reading with an open mind, and then deciding what to believe or do (Ennis, 1989). Critical readers can identify the author's purpose and point of view as well as distinguish fact from opinion (Roe, Stoodt, & Burns, 1998). Critical reading raises students' awareness that all texts are written by ordinary people with their own attitudes and understandings of the world. This empowers students to question and challenge the author and deepens engagement in the text.

Question the author also raises students' awareness of the writer behind the text. Using this approach, students continually ask themselves, "What does the author mean?" (Beck, McKeown, Hamilton, & Kucan, 1997; Beck, McKeown, Worthy, Sandora, & Kucan, 1996). Readers update their hypotheses about the text as they progress. The interactions that occur between students and text enhance engagement and comprehension.

Beck, I. L., McKeown, M. G., Worthy J., Sandora, C. A., & Kucan, L. (1996). Questioning the author: A yearlong classroom implementation to engage students with text. *Elementary School Journal*, 96, 385-414.

Beck, I. L., McKeown, M. G., Hamilton, R., & Kucan, L. (1997). *Questioning the author: An approach for enhancing student engagement with text*. Newark, DE: International Reading Association

Brown, A. L., & Day, J. D. (1983). Macrorules for summarizing texts: The development of expertise. *Journal of Verbal Learning and Verbal Behavior*, 22, 1-14.

Dana, C. (1989). Strategy families for disabled readers. *Journal of Reading*, 33, 30-35.

Ennis, R. (1989). Critical thinking and subject specificity: Clarification and needed research. *Educational Researcher*, 18, 4-10.

Heilman, A. W., Blair, T. R., & Rupley, W. H. (2002). *Principles and practices of teaching reading* (10th ed.). Upper Saddle River, NJ: Merrill Prentice Hall.

Roe, B. D., Stoodt, B. D., & Burns, P. C. (1998). *The content areas: Secondary school literacy instruction* (6th ed.). Boston: Houghton Mifflin.

Reading Fiction

Chapter 6 provides strategies for reading literature that can help adolescents make the transition from children's and young adult literature to the more demanding study of canonized adult literature. To be successful comprehenders of such literature, students need a good grasp of theme, characterization, setting, and plot.

Understanding the basic form and variations of plot structure enables students to comprehend and recall stories. Traditional plots include exposition, rising action, a climax, falling action, and a resolution. When readers use their knowledge of story structure, they are better able to retain information in their memory until it makes sense and to add information as they read (Gordon & Braun, 1983).

Graphic organizers are widely used to reinforce students' comprehension of basic story structure as well as help them analyze particular stories (e.g., Cooper, 2000). As with expository texts, using graphic organizers focuses students' attention on the most important aspects of narratives. Simple graphic organizers, such as the Story String or Storyboard, help students sort and organize key events. Other popular graphic organizers for literature are the Character Map, Fiction Organizer, Setting Chart, Plot Diagram, and Topic and Theme Organizer.

Synthesizing is another essential strategy for reading literature successfully at the high school level. Synthesizing involves gathering the important parts of a work of literature and fitting them together, like a puzzle, to show the "big picture." Synthesizing enables students to make reasonable hypotheses about themes in literature, which is a skill that becomes increasingly important in higher level literature classes (Phelan, 1989).

Cooper, J. D. (2000). *Literacy: Helping children construct meaning* (4th ed.). Boston: Houghton Mifflin.

Gordon, C. J., & Braun, C. (1983). Using story schema as an aid to reading and writing. *The Reading Teacher*, 2, 116-121.

Phelan, J. (1989). *Reading people, reading plots: Character, progression, and the interpretation of narrative*. Chicago: University of Chicago Press.

Reading Poetry

Many high school students have difficulty reading and interpreting poetry. As in the preceding chapter, the strategies in Chapter 7 are designed to facilitate students' transition to the more demanding study of poetry in the higher grades.

Poetry, like other forms of literature, is meant to evoke personal feelings and thoughts in readers. Valuing students' personal responses to poetry and other literature is essential for fostering an appreciation of and interest in literature. Reader response theory, especially as elaborated by Louise Rosenblatt (1978), has legitimized the role of individual, subjective thoughts and feelings in the study of poetry and literature.

Though the reader's subjective responses are an essential part of literary interpretation (Rosenblatt, 1978), this does not mean "anything goes." Careful attention to the words, images, patterns, and structure of a poem is also essential. The *Reader's Handbook* presents the strategy of close reading to scaffold students' careful readings of a poem. Students are instructed not only to read "word by word and line by line," but also to read the poem multiple times to facilitate close reading.

The handbook unites reader response and close reading in the Double-entry Journal tool (Berthoff, 1981). In this organizer, a notebook page is divided into two columns, and students record quotations from the poem in the first column and their personal thoughts and feelings about the quotations in the second. Double-entry Journals have been found to be effective with all students, including those at risk (Coley & Hoffman, 1990).

Paraphrasing is another useful strategy that helps adolescents better understand poetry. When students rewrite lines of a poem in their own words, students begin to see action and characterization. Paraphrasing encourages active reading and student response to literature (Roe, Stoodt, & Burns, 1998).

Berthoff, A. E. (1981). *The making of meaning*. Montclair, NJ: Boynton/Cook.

Coley, J. D., & Hoffman, D. M. (1990). Overcoming learned helplessness in at-risk readers. *Journal of Reading*, 33, 497-502.

Roe, B. D., Stoodt, B. D., & Burns, P. C. (1998). *The content areas: Secondary school literacy instruction* (6th ed.), Boston: Houghton Mifflin.

Rosenblatt, L. M. (1978). *The reader, the text, the poem: The transactional theory of the literary work*. Carbondale, IL: Southern Illinois University Press.

Reading Drama

Reading drama may also be difficult for adolescents. Drama has several features that make it different from other literary forms and difficult to read (Roe, Stoodt, and Burns, 1998). For example, plays include no detailed narrative descriptions of characters or setting. The story is conveyed solely through dialogue. Also unique in plays is the stage direction—all in italics and parentheses—which must be read and comprehended to understand character motivation and plot. Chapter 8 provides strategies and tools that help high school students read and understand drama.

Summarizing while reading a play enables students to keep track of the characters and action. Summarizing involves pulling together the main elements in a text and is a key strategy of effective readers (Cooper, 2000). Providing guidelines can help students develop this strategy (Brown & Day, 1983). The Magnet Summary graphic organizer presented in the handbook provides the structure necessary for students to develop or improve their summarizing abilities.

Brown, A. L., & Day, J. D. (1983). Macrorules for summarizing texts: The development of expertise. *Journal of Verbal Learning and Verbal Behavior, 22*, 1-14.

Cooper, J. D. (2000). *Literacy: Helping children construct meaning* (4th ed.). Boston: Houghton Mifflin.

Roe, B. D., Stoodt, B. D., & Burns, P. C. (1998). *The content areas: Secondary school literacy instruction* (6th ed.), Boston: Houghton Mifflin.

Reading the Internet

Chapter 9 provides strategies to help students read on the Internet. Though the Internet is a valuable source of information for students (Troutner, 2000), Internet reading poses challenges that many educators do not yet fully appreciate. For example, although reading email usually does not differ greatly from reading a letter on paper, reading a website is extremely different from reading a book chapter. In website reading, the eye jumps from one spot to another, in any direction. Adolescents can easily get lost or sidetracked while reading a website.

Students who are first learning about the Internet may experience "information overload" (Hawes, 1998). Instruction in how to analyze the information found on the Internet is necessary. Hawes (1998) recommends a list of questions, including questions about the authors' points of view, authors' purposes, and authors' proofs for their viewpoints, all of which promote critical reading.

Ryder and Graves (1997) concur that critical thinking is an essential skill for successful Internet use. The Internet's vast amount of readily accessible information is an advantage but comes at the cost of being largely unrestricted. The challenge is to "make qualitative judgments as to the accuracy and reliability" of this information (Ryder & Graves, 1997).

The handbook stresses the need for critical reading of information on the Internet. Critical reading is the ability to evaluate the material for accuracy, bias, and reliability. Reflecting, suspending judgment initially, and deciding what to believe are essential components (Ennis, 1989). Students who read critically are alert to the author's purpose and distinguish between fact and opinion (Roe, Stoodt, & Burns, 1998). The handbook scaffolds high school students' ability to critically read Internet material.

Ennis, R. (1989). Critical thinking and subject specificity: Clarification and needed research. *Educational Researcher, 18*, 4-10.

Hawes, K .S. (1998). Reading the Internet: Conducting research for the virtual classroom. *Journal of Adolescent and Adult Literacy, 41*, 563-566.

Roe, B. D., Stoodt, B. D., & Burns, P. C. (1998). *The content areas: Secondary school literacy instruction* (6th ed.), Boston: Houghton Mifflin.

Ryder, R. J., & Graves, M. F. (1997). Using the Internet to enhance students' reading, writing, and information-gathering skills. *Journal of Adolescent and Adult Literacy, 40*, 244-254.

Troutner, J. (2000). Web wonders. *Teacher Librarian, 27*, 39-42.

Reading Graphics

Helping students learn to read graphics is an important goal in literacy instruction (Fry, 1981). Content area textbooks contain a variety of graphic types (Roe, Stoodt, & Burns, 1998). Because graphics are abstract and often oversimplify or appear to distort information, deciphering them can be confusing (Roe, et al., 1998). However, the need to accurately read graphics is likely to become increasingly important. Chapter 10 provides strategies that enable high school students to read charts, graphs, tables, and diagrams in their textbooks and in other sources.

Paraphrasing is a useful strategy for reading graphics. This skill requires students to think about the information in the graphics and translate it into their own words. Research shows that paraphrasing increases students' comprehension and recall of content area material (Shugarman & Hurst, 1986). Students need support, as is provided in the handbook, to learn this skill (Roe, et al., 1998).

Fry, E. (1981). Graphical literacy. *Journal of Reading*, 24, 383-390.

Roe, B. D., Stoodt, B. D., & Burns, P. C. (1998). *The content areas*: *Secondary school literacy instruction*, (6th ed). Boston: Houghton Mifflin.

Shugarman, S. L., & Hurst, J. B. (1986). Purposeful paraphrasing: Promoting a nontrivial pursuit for meaning. *Journal of Reading*, 29, 396-399.

Reading for the Everyday World

"Real-world" reading becomes increasingly important during adolescence. In Chapter 11, the Handbook presents lessons on reading a driver's handbook, with focus sections on reading for work and reading instructions. The strategies presented to help students effectively read materials in the everyday world are skimming, close-reading, and visualizing and thinking aloud.

Skimming is a type of rapid reading done to get an overview or gist of the material (Roe, Stoodt, & Burns, 1998). It is one method for increasing adolescents' reading rate and flexibility, enabling students to cover large amounts of text in the shortest time possible (Roe, et al., 1998). It also provides readers with enough information about the material to generate their own purposes for reading (Jacobowitz, 1988).

As in other handbook lessons, the structured note-taking techniques provided enable students to identify important information (Smith & Tompkins, 1988). Because students are asked to record textual information in graphic organizers, they must identify the most important information, which improves comprehension and recall (Alvermann & Moore, 1991; Anderson & Armbruster, 1984).

Visualizing and thinking aloud are also useful comprehension strategies for high school students (Vacca & Vacca, 2002). Visualizing, which helps adolescents to connect with the text, promotes engagement (Wilhelm, 1997). Thinking aloud helps students work through problems with the text and facilitates recall of textual information (Jacobowitz, 1988).

Alvermann, D.E., & Moore, D.W. (1991). Secondary schools. In R. Barr, M.L. Kamil, P.B. Mosenthal, & P.D. Pearson (Eds.), *Handbook of reading research* (Vol. 2, pp. 951-983). New York: Longman.

Anderson, T.H., & Armbruster, B.B. (1984). Studying. In P.D. Pearson (Ed.), *Handbook of reading research* (pp. 657-679). New York: Longman.

Jacobowitz, T. (1988). Using therapy to modify practice: An illustration with SQ3R. *Journal of Reading*, 32, 126-131.

Smith, P.L., & Tompkins, G.E. (1988). Structured notetaking: A new strategy for content area readers. *Journal of Reading*, 32, 46-53.

Roe, B.D., Stoodt, B.D., & Burns, P.C. (1998). *The content areas: Secondary school literacy instruction*, (6th ed.). Boston: Houghton Mifflin.

Vacca, R.T., & Vacca., J.L. (2002). *Content area reading: Literacy and learning across the curriculum* (7th ed.). Boston: Allyn & Bacon.

Wilhelm, J. (1997). *"You gotta BE the book": Teaching engaged and reflective reading with adolescents.* New York: Teachers College Press.

Reading for Tests

The reading required for tests presents a unique set of challenges for adolescents. Sometimes high school students do poorly on tests, not because they didn't study, but because they had problems comprehending test questions and directions (Roe, Stoodt, & Burns, 1998). Chapter 12 discusses how students can best prepare for tests and provides useful strategies for helping students successfully read test directions and questions.

Additional challenges to reading on tests include students' own feelings of anxiety, which are distracting and hinder comprehension. No matter what type of test the student is taking, time is limited. Students must be able to understand what the questions are asking quickly and precisely. Some tests require students to read, comprehend, and answer questions on new material. On multiple-choice tests, students must read and understand all possible answers. In addition, question types vary from one test to another, as do instructions on how to answer the questions.

The handbook presents strategies for students to succeed on standardized tests as well as on English, writing, history, math, and science tests. Using a sample from a standardized test, students practice skimming a passage to find answers to the questions that follow it. In addition, Chapter 12 discusses three basic question types—factual/recall, critical thinking, and essay. Educators have found that, when students understand the relationship between questions and answers, they tend to perform better on tests (Raphael, 1984, 1986; Vacca & Vacca, 2002).

Raphael, T. E. (1984). Teaching learners about sources of information for answering comprehension questions. *Journal of Reading*, 27, 303-311.

Raphael, T. E. (1986). Reaching question-answer relationships. *Reading Teacher*, 39, 516-520.

Roe, B.D., Stoodt, B.D., & Burns, P.C. (1998). *The content areas: Secondary school literacy instruction*, (6th ed.). Boston: Houghton Mifflin.

Vacca, R. T., & Vacca, J. L. (2002). *Content area reading: Literacy and learning across the curriculum* (7th ed.). Boston: Allyn & Bacon.

Improving Vocabulary

Chapter 13 focuses on ways for high school students to increase their vocabulary knowledge. Knowledge of word meanings is strongly associated with reading comprehension (Anderson & Freebody, 1981; Davis, 1971). However, improving vocabulary knowledge and comprehension requires much more than simply teaching a few words from the material before a reading (Nagy, 1988).

Research on how students acquire vocabulary is extensive (Beck & McKeown, 1991). Findings show that vocabulary knowledge develops through wide reading (Fielding, Wilson, & Anderson, 1986; Nagy & Herman, 1987); that students benefit from instruction on how to use context clues to infer word meanings (Jenkins, Stein, & Wysocki, 1984; Sternberg, 1987); and that dictionary skills are needed (Schatz & Baldwin, 1986).

The handbook encourages students to become active word learners. Seven ways to learn new words are suggested: keeping a vocabulary journal, looking up new words, pronouncing words, keeping a file box, learning words every day, using new words, and creating concept Maps. The handbook also explains how to effectively use context clues, in accord with research showing that students need a good grasp of strategies for independently inferring word meanings from context (e.g., Graves, 1987). The handbook provides authentic text examples of context clues, rather than contrived passages that can give students an unrealistic idea of how easy this process is.

Because learning how to use context clues alone is not enough to build vocabulary (Schatz & Baldwin, 1986), the handbook also covers dictionary and thesaurus skills. Other approaches found to be beneficial and included in the handbook are word analysis skills (e.g., Rupley & Blair, 1988) and graphic organizers for word leaning (e.g., Cooper, 2000).

Anderson, R. C., & Freebody, P. (1981). Vocabulary knowledge. In J. T. Guthrie (Ed.), *Comprehension and teaching: Research reviews*. Newark, DE: International Reading Association.

Beck, I. L., & McKeown, M. G. (1991). Conditions of vocabulary acquisition. In R. Barr, M. L. Kamil, P. Mosenthal, & P. D. Pearson (Eds.), *Handbook of reading research,* (Vol. 2, pp. 789-814). New York: Longman.

Cooper, J. D. (2000). *Literacy: Helping children construct meaning* (4th ed.). Boston: Houghton Mifflin.

Davis, F. (1971). Psychometric research in reading comprehension. In F. Davis (Ed.), *Literature of research in reading with emphasis on models*. Brunswick, NJ: Rutgers University Press.

Fielding, L. G., Wilson, P. T., & Anderson, R. C. (1986). A new focus on free reading: The role of tradebooks in reading instruction. In T. E. Raphael (Ed.), *Contexts of school-based literacy*, pp. 149-160. New York: Random House.

Graves, M. F. (1987). The roles of instruction in fostering vocabulary development. In M. G. McKeown & M. E. Curtis (Eds.), *The nature of vocabulary acquisition* (pp. 165-184). Hillsdale, NJ: Lawrence Erlbaum.

Jenkins, J. R., Stein, M., & Wysocki, K. (1984). Learning vocabulary through reading. *American Education Research Journal,* 21, 767-788.

Nagy, W. E. (1988). *Teaching vocabulary to improve reading comprehension*. Newark, DE: International Reading Association.

Nagy, W. E., & Herman, P. A. (1987). Breadth and depth of vocabulary knowledge: Implications for acquisition and instruction. In M. G. McKeown & M. E. Curtis (Eds.), *The nature of vocabulary acquisition* (pp. 19-35). Hillsdale, NJ: Lawrence Erlbaum.

Rupley, W. H., Logan, J. W., & Nichols, W. D. (1999). Vocabulary instruction in a balanced reading program. *The Reading Teacher,* 52, 338-347.

Schatz, E. K., & Baldwin, R. S. (1986). Context clues are unreliable predictors of word meanings. *Reading Research Quarterly,* 21, 439-453.

Sternberg, R. J. (1987). Most vocabulary is learned from context. In M. G. McKeown & M. E. Curtis (Eds.), *The nature of vocabulary acquisition* (pp. 89-105). Hillsdale, NJ: Lawrence Erlbaum.

Reader's Almanac

The *Reader's Handbook* concludes with a "Reader's Almanac," which reviews the strategies and their uses. With concise definitions and explanations of when to use the strategies, the Almanac serves as a useful quick reference, enabling students to independently review key strategies.

In addition to the strategy review, the Almanac provides a list and review of "reading tools"—different types of graphic organizers and note-taking techniques that scaffold students' comprehension and ability to recall the information they read. These tools include research-supported methods such as Double-entry Journals (Berthoff, 1981) and Webs (Bromley, 1996).

Research shows that good comprehenders are strategic readers who adjust their reading according to purpose and text type (Anderson, Hiebert, Scott,& Wilkinson, 1985). Expert readers use a variety of strategies to construct meaning before, during, and after reading (Paris, Wasik, & Turner, 1991). Students who lack knowledge of or ability to use strategies —who feel unable to overcome problems encountered while reading—are at risk for low achievement (Vacca & Padak, 1990). To succeed in reading, adolescents need a good grasp of a variety of strategies to help them learn from text. The Reader's Handbook puts key strategies within the reach of all high school students.

Anderson, R. C., Hiebert, E. H., Scott, J. A., & Wilkinson, I. A. G. (1985). *Becoming a nation of readers*. Washington. DC: National Institute of Education.

Berthoff, A. E. (1981). *The making of meaning*. Montclair, NJ: Boynton/Cook.

Bromley, K. D. (1996). *Webbing with literature: Creating story maps with children's books*. Boston: Allyn & Bacon.

Paris, S. G., Wasik, B. A., & Turner, J. C. (1991). The development of strategic readers. In R. Barr, M. L. Kamil, P. Mosenthal, & P. D. Pearson (Eds.), *Handbook of reading research,* (Vol. 2, pp. 609-640). New York: Longman.

Vacca, R. T., & Padak, N. D. (1990). Who's at risk in reading? *Journal of Reading, 33,* 486-489.

Introduction

For use with pages 15–35

Daily Lessons	Summary
Lesson 1 **What Is the *Reader's Handbook?***	Explore with students the goals of the *Reader's Handbook* Help students personalize these goals to reflect their own needs.
Lesson 2 **How to Use the Handbook**	Explain key elements of the handbook and how students can use them over the course of the year.
Lesson 3 **Reflecting on Reading**	Refine students' understanding of what happens when you read.
Lesson 4 **Reading as a Process**	Work with students to help them understand reading as a process. Compare the reading process to the more familiar writing process.

Lesson Resources

Overheads
For this lesson, use:
Overhead 1: Reading Process

See *Student Applications Book 10* pages 6–11

See *Teacher's Guide* pp. 29–38

See *Test Book* for multiple-choice and short-answer tests.

See Website www.greatsource.com/rehand

For more practice, see also *Sourcebook* Grade 10, pages 7–10. *Daybook* Grade 10, pages 9–20.

WEEK 2
The Reading Process

For use with *Reader's Handbook* pages 26–43

Daily Lessons	Summary
Lesson 1 **The Reading Process:** **An Overview**	Offer a detailed introduction to the reading process. Present an overview of the three stages of the process and the two or three steps in each stage.
Lesson 2 **The Before** **Reading Stage**	Explain the Before Reading stage. Introduce several of the reading strategies students will learn about over the course of the year.
Lesson 3 **The During** **Reading Stage**	Examine with students the During Reading stage of the reading process and the variety of tools they can use to keep track of their thoughts and ideas as they read.
Lesson 4 **The After** **Reading Stage**	Walk through the final stage of the reading process. Help students understand the importance of reflecting upon, rereading, and remembering a text.

Lesson Resources

Overheads

For this lesson, use:
Overhead 1: Reading Process

See *Student Applications Book 10* pages 10–11.

See *Teacher's Guide* pages 34–38.

See *Test Book* for multiple-choice and short-answer tests.

See Website www.greatsource.com/rehand

For more practice, see also *Sourcebook* Grade 10, pages 9–10; *Daybook* Grade 10, page 11.

WEEK 1
Lesson 1
What Is the *Reader's Handbook?*

For use with *Reader's Handbook* pages 15–18

Goals

In this lesson, students explore the goals and purposes of the *Reader's Handbook*.

Teaching Focus

Background

The *Reader's Handbook* incorporates years of educational research. Its primary goal is to give students an easy, effective reading process that they can use with all kinds of texts. The reading process presented in the handbook may be similar to one you've already taught your students. If so, use the handbook to reinforce your teaching. If the process is new to students, however, use the handbook as your primary teaching tool. Begin by exploring the steps in the reading process and then use those steps with various types of writing.

Instruction

Ask students to define the word *handbook*. Point out that the *Reader's Handbook* can be a textbook, a practice book, or a reference book, depending on students' needs. Then discuss the goals of the handbook. Students should know that most important goal is to help then become more proficient readers. Have students compare that goal with their own reading and learning goals.

Teaching Approach

Use of the Handbook

Have a student volunteer read aloud the unit opener on page 15. As a class, read and discuss the information on pages 16–18. Talk about the three goals of the *Reader's Handbook*. Then have students meet in groups and suggest possible uses of the handbook. Come together as a class and share how you envision the class will use the handbook.

Extend the Handbook

Have students begin reading journals that they will use throughout their work with the handbook. Have students begin their journals by listing their personal goals for using the *Reader's Handbook*. Invite students to share their goals. Describe your goals for the class as well.

Assessment

Ask students:

■ What is the one thing you hope to gain from using the *Reader's Handbook?*

■ What are some of the ways you can see to use the handbook?

WEEK 1
Lesson 2 — How to Use the Handbook

For use with *Reader's Handbook* pages 19–23

Goals

In this lesson, students learn the four major parts of the *Reader's Handbook* and discuss how to use each.

Teaching Focus

Background

Invite students who are familiar with the handbook to thumb through its pages, marking with stickies those sections about which they have lingering questions. For those students who are using the handbook for the first time, present a detailed lesson on how the book is organized and how each part of the book can improve students' reading (and thinking) skills.

Instruction

First, have students examine the handbook's Table of Contents (pages 13–14). Ask them which features stand out and whether they noticed any organizational patterns. Then explain that the handbook has four main parts: the reading lessons, the focus lessons, Elements mini-lessons, and the almanac. Let students know that the majority of the teaching is done in the reading lessons. In the focus lessons, students explore certain smaller aspects of the main reading lesson. Then discuss the purpose of the Elements sections and how you plan to use them. Do the same for the Reader's Almanac.

Teaching Approach

Use of the Handbook

First, point out that the *Reader's Handbook* has its own structure and that by examining the way it is organized, students will be better equipped to use it effectively. Then have students read pages 19–23. Pause after each of the four sections to discuss. Have students summarize the purpose of the section and think about how it might be used. Then have students skim the rest of the handbook to look for specific examples of the key features discussed on pages 19–23.

Extend the Handbook

Have students reflect on this lesson in their reading journals. Ask them to describe what they learned from their previews and predict whether the handbook can help them meet the goals they listed in the previous lesson.

Assessment

Ask students:

- What is the purpose of the *Reader's Handbook?*
- Why do you need a reading handbook if you already know how to read?
- What would you most like to improve about your reading habits?

Reflecting on Reading

WEEK 1
Lesson 3

For use with *Reader's Handbook* pages 26–29

Goals

In this lesson, students expand their understanding of what reading is and why reading is such an important skill.

Teaching Focus

Background

Students should know that reading is more than just decoding the words on a page. Reading is also about extracting meaning and making personal connections to a text. Most important of all, reading is about thinking in an organized, effective manner—hopefully through the use of a process similar to the one described in the *Reader's Handbook*. The handbook's process facilitates students' metacognitive awareness of their strengths and weaknesses as readers. This lesson begins the facilitation by inviting students to take the time to reflect on reading. Here you'll ask students the all-important questions: What is reading? How does it work? and Why do we do it?

Instruction

Open with a question: What is reading? Ask students to quickwrite their answers in their reading journals. (Be sure to point out that there may be many different answers to the question.) Then have student volunteers share their quickwrites. Work together as a class to come up with a definition for reading. Compare the class definition to the definition given in the handbook on pages 26–27. Repeat the activities with two additional questions: Why do you read? and What do you read?

Teaching Approach

Use of the Handbook

After the class brainstorms a definition for reading, have them read silently the information on page 26 and the top of page 27. Ask students, How does this information compare with the class definition of reading? Next, have students read the remainder of page 27 and all of page 28. Invite students to comment on the quotes in the middle of the page. Then have students read and reflect on page 29. Ask students, How did this section of the handbook affect your understanding of reading? For additional practice, see pages 6–9 of *Student Applications Book 10*.

Extend the Handbook

Ask students to reread the question on page 28 and then list ten reasons of their own for reading. Have them rank the reasons in order of importance.

Assessment

Ask students:

- Why is reading important?

- How would you explain what reading is to someone who has never experienced it?

WEEK 1
Lesson 4 Reading as a Process

For use with *Reader's Handbook* pages 30–35

Goals

In this lesson, you'll help students begin to think of reading as a process, rather than a single, finite event.

Teaching Focus

Background

It makes sense to think of reading as a process, but students rarely do. Instead, they assume that reading begins with the first word and ends with the last. In this lesson, you'll help students take their first step in learning to think of reading as a process. Connecting the reading process to the more familiar writing process will provide a framework for building students' understanding.

Instruction

Review the steps of the writing process by having students list them on the board. Discuss how each step helps students meet the goal of writing well. Then explain that proficient readers follow a similar process when they read. Ask students to predict what steps are involved in the reading process. For those students who have learned the reading process before, see how many of the steps they can correctly recall.

Teaching Approach

Use of the Handbook

Have students read page 33 in the *Reader's Handbook* independently. As a class, discuss the information, especially the idea that reading is like creating a "first draft" of your understanding. Then direct students' attention to the comparison between the reading and writing processes. Help students see that when they read, they make decisions in the same way they make decisions while writing. Finish the lesson by reading aloud the final paragraph on page 35. Ask for questions and comments.

Extend the Handbook

To end this introductory section, have students reflect on their own experiences as readers. Questions they might consider: How would I rate myself as a reader? Why? What is my greatest reading strength? What is my most worrisome weakness?

Assessment

Ask students:

■ What are some important elements of reading?

■ What is the connection between the reading and writing processes?

■ What have you learned about yourself as a reader from working though this section of the *Reader's Handbook?*

WEEK 2
Lesson 1

The Reading Process: An Overview

For use with *Reader's Handbook* pages 26–43

Goals

In this lesson, students learn about the reading process and how they can use it to improve their understanding of written texts.

Teaching Focus

Background

Understanding how the reading process works and why it is effective is an important first step in teaching students to become more proficient readers. In this lesson, you'll introduce the process and provide a brief overview of the three stages of the process: Before Reading, During Reading, and After Reading. In addition, you'll help students understand that they can use the reading process with a variety of texts, including fiction, nonfiction, textbooks, test passages, and so on.

Instruction

Begin with a discussion of the process students currently use when reading. What do they do before, during, and after reading a novel, for example, or a school textbook? Next, explain that the *Reader's Handbook* offers a reading process that may differ slightly from the one students are using. Then move on to a specific discussion of the handbook's reading process. Explain the three distinct stages. Point out that each stage is broken down into two or three steps.

Teaching Focus

Use of the Handbook

As a warm-up activity, ask students to work in small groups to read pages 26–29. Have each group discuss what reading is and individual group members' reading likes and dislikes. Then ask the groups to explore the information about effective and ineffective readers on pages 30–32. Finish the lesson by walking through with students the steps of the reading process, beginning on page 38.

Extend the Handbook

Explain the importance of developing a shared vocabulary of reading terms that the whole class can understand and call upon when discussing reading. Have students devote a section of their reading journals to vocabulary they learn in the *Reader's Handbook*. Remind them to add to their vocabulary lists over the course of the year.

Assessment

Ask students:

■ What is a reading process and why do you need one?

■ What are the three stages of the reading process presented in the *Reader's Handbook?*

WEEK 2
Lesson 2 · The Before Reading Stage

For use with *Reader's Handbook* pages 38–39

Goals

In this lesson, students will learn about and then discuss the three steps of the Before Reading stage of the reading process. In addition, they'll explore several of the reading strategies presented in the *Reader's Handbook*.

Teaching Focus

Background

Reading anxiety often stems from not knowing what to expect or anticipating that the assigned text will be too hard, too complicated, or too boring. Model for students how to use the Before Reading stage of the process to allay fears about reading. Explain that setting a purpose beforehand can make it easier to concentrate at the During Reading stage. Previewing can give readers an idea of what to expect and may give them a more realistic sense of the difficulty level of the text. Making a plan can also help readers feel more in control of the assignment.

Instruction

Begin by drawing an analogy between the Before Reading stage of the reading process and the warm-up exercises an athlete performs before a competition. Like an athlete, a reader must prepare for the challenge to come. Then begin exploring the individual steps of the Before Reading stage: Set a Purpose, Preview, and Plan.

Teaching Approach

Use of the Handbook

Ask volunteers to read the text under the heads Set a Purpose, Preview, and Plan. After they've finished, summarize for the class how each step works and why it is important. Ask students, Which of these steps is familiar to you? Have you ever set a purpose or previewed a text ahead of time? End the lesson by drawing students' attention to the Strategy Handbook (pages 713–737) and discussing several of the key strategies. Explain that, over the course of the year, students will learn how to use each of the strategies shown.

Extend the Handbook

Have students summarize the purpose of the Before Reading stage of the reading process and then discuss each of the three steps. They can write their summaries in their reading journals or present them orally in small groups.

For additional practice, ask students to complete pages 10–11 of *Student Applications Book 10*.

Assessment

Ask students:

■ What are the three steps of the Before Reading stage of the reading process?

■ What is the purpose of each step?

WEEK 2
Lesson 3
The During Reading Stage

For use with *Reader's Handbook* pages 40–41

Goals

In this lesson, students explore the During Reading stage of the reading process and discuss how using a specific reading strategy can help them get more from a text.

Teaching Focus

Background

The During Reading stage involves more than simply reading the text. Keep in mind that your goal is to help students become more active readers. This means, then, that students should think of the During Reading stage as their time to ask questions of the author, comment on what he or she has said, and relate the text to their own lives. Reiterate that the reading strategy they've chosen at the Before Reading stage can help them read actively.

Instruction

Discuss the importance of what it means to be an active, as opposed to a passive, reader. Have students tell active reading techniques that they currently use, and then work with them to compare the techniques to those described in the *Reader's Handbook*. During the second half of the lesson, explore the two steps of the During Reading stage: Read with a Purpose and Connect. Explain how keeping an eye on the original reading purpose can help students stay centered as they read. Point out that proficient readers know how to modify their purpose as needed or change it completely if the text doesn't support the original purpose. Explain that connecting a text with their lives will help then see its relevance and help maintain interest.

Teaching Approach

Use of the Handbook

Read aloud the text under Read with a Purpose on page 40. Emphasize the importance of paying careful attention to facts and details in the text that speak to that purpose. Next, have students read silently the paragraph under the head Connect. Ask students to read the four connect questions shown and then think about other questions they could ask themselves when relating a text to their lives.

Extend the Handbook

Once again, ask students to complete a written or oral summary of this stage of the reading process. Ask students, How will the During Reading stage work for you?

Assessment

Ask students:

■ What are the two steps of the During Reading stage of the reading process?

■ What does it mean to read with a purpose?

■ How does a reader connect to a text?

The After Reading Stage

For use with *Reader's Handbook* pages 41–43

Goals

In this lesson, students learn about the final stage of the reading process, After Reading, and why it is important to reflect upon a text.

Teaching Focus

Background

Help students understand that the reading process doesn't stop as soon as they finish the article, story, or poem. There is one final stage that occurs *after* the last word has been read. It is at this point that students should reflect upon the meaning of the text, whether they've met their purpose, and techniques they'll use to remember what they've read.

Instruction

Ask students what they usually do after they finish a book. Do they spend time thinking about what they've read, or do they wipe it out of their minds as quickly as possible? After your discussion, explain how important it is to think about a reading once you've finished it. Explore what it means to reflect on a text and the questions students might ask themselves at this stage in the process. Then explain that often students will find that they need to reread a text, sometimes more than once. When this is the case, they should choose a rereading strategy that they think will work with that particular piece of literature.

Teaching Approach

Use of the Handbook

Have students read silently pages 41–43. Discuss the Pause and Reflect and Reread steps and how they might be modified for different kinds of texts. Ask students, Why do you think the Reread stage is particularly important with poetry? or Why is the Remember stage so important with a textbook? Discuss techniques students currently use to remember what they've read. Point out that writing a fact or idea can make it easier to remember and that graphic organizers (such as those shown in the Reading Tools section) are like word pictures that students can "draw" and commit to memory.

Extend the Handbook

If students will benefit from additional practice with the reading process, have them complete pages 10–11 of *Student Applications Book 10.*

Assessment

Ask students:

■ Why is it important to pause and reflect after reading?

■ How can you use the reading process to help you become a better reader?

WEEK 3
Reading Know-how

For use with *Reader's Handbook* pages 46–52

Daily Lessons	Summary
Lesson 1 **Reading Know-how:** **An Overview**	Introduce four critical thinking skills that proficient readers use with every text.
Lesson 2 **Making Inferences** **and Drawing Conclusions**	Discuss how and why readers make inferences and draw conclusions.
Lesson 3 **Comparing,** **Contrasting, and** **Evaluating**	Activate prior knowledge of comparing and contrasting. Discuss the importance of evaluating a text.
Lesson 4 **Reading Actively**	Teach the importance of reading actively.

Lesson Resources

See *Student Applications Book 10* pages 12–14.

See *Teacher's Guide* pages 40–43.

See *Test Book* for multiple-choice and short-answer tests.

See Website www.greatsource.com/rehand

For more practice, see also *Sourcebook* Grade 9, pages 8–10; *Daybook* Grade 10, pages 22–25.

WEEK 4

Reading Paragraphs

For use with *Reader's Handbook* pages 53–69

Daily Lessons	Summary
Lesson 1 **Finding the Subject of a Paragraph**	Present an overview of the characteristics of a paragraph. Explain how to identify the writer's subject.
Lesson 2 **Finding the Main Idea**	Discuss with the class how to find the main idea of a paragraph.
Lesson 3 **Types of Paragraphs**	Explore four types of paragraphs: narrative, descriptive, expository, and persuasive.
Lesson 4 **Ways of Organizing Paragraphs**	Build understanding of the arrangement of details in a paragraph. Discuss eight common ways of organizing a paragraph.

Lesson Resources

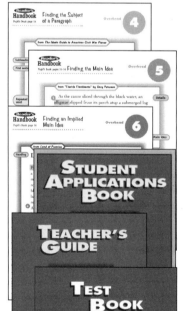

Overheads

For this lesson, use:
Overhead 4: Finding the Subject of a Paragraph
Overhead 5: Finding the Main Idea
Overhead 6: Finding the Implied Main Idea

See *Student Applications Book 10* pages 17–19.

See *Teacher's Guide* pages 42–43.

See *Test Book* for multiple-choice and short-answer tests.

See Website www.greatsource.com/rehand

For more practice, see also *Sourcebook*
Grade 10, pages 12–19; *Daybook*
Grade 10, pages 98–99.

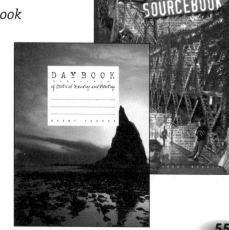

Reading Know-how: An Overview

WEEK 3
Lesson 1

For use with *Reader's Handbook* pages 46–47

Goals

Here you'll present an introduction to four essential thinking skills: making inferences, drawing conclusions, comparing and contrasting, and evaluating.

Teaching Focus

Background

Proficient readers know how to think critically. They move beyond the literal meaning of the words on a page and make inferences about what those words mean. Using such critical thinking skills as making inferences, drawing conclusions, comparing and contrasting, and evaluating is an essential part of a student's reading foundation.

Instruction

Begin your lesson by writing the following scenario on the board: *A school bus with the words* Philadelphia Public School District *written on its side picks up a group of students and then follows signs that say* Shore Points. Have students read the scenario and discuss the literal meaning of the words. Then explain that they can use critical thinking skills to read between the lines in the scenario. Ask students, Where is the bus going? Where is it coming from? What is the purpose of the trip? To answer these questions, students need to make inferences and draw conclusions. During the second half of the lesson, post a different scenario on the board and help students use the critical thinking skill of evaluating to read between the lines.

Teaching Approach

Use of the Handbook

Ask a student volunteer to read aloud the opening paragraph on page 46. Discuss the foundation of a house analogy. Then identify the four critical thinking skills you'll be discussing over the course of the week. Have students preview pages 46–52 in preparation for the work ahead.

Extend the Handbook

To give students additional practice with the four critical thinking skills, have them complete pages 12–13 of *Student Applications Book 10*.

Assessment

Ask students:

■ What does it mean to "read between the lines"?

■ What "know-how" do you use to become a better reader?

Making Inferences and Drawing Conclusions

For use with *Reader's Handbook* pages 46–47

Goals

In this lesson, students learn the importance of using the critical thinking skills of making inferences and drawing conclusions.

Teaching Focus

Background

When you make inferences, you make reasonable guesses about what something means. For example, if you see a dog wagging its tail, you can make the inference that the dog is happy. Drawing conclusions means gathering bits of information and then deciding what that information means. These two critical thinking skills help readers move beyond the literal understanding of a text. More proficient readers make inferences and draw conclusions automatically as they read. Struggling readers may need some help understanding how to use these skills.

Instruction

Begin by asking students to explain what it means to make inferences and draw conclusions. Then have a volunteer provide an example of each skill. Point out that students' own knowledge and experiences—along with the information provided— enables them to make an inference or draw a conclusion.

Teaching Approach

Use of the Handbook

Open by having students read silently the information about making inferences on page 46. Copy the "inference equation" onto the board and have students practice using it to make inferences. Then have the class turn to page 47. Once again, draw students' attention to the equation in the center of the page. Explain that in a longer text, they may find scads of "information" that they can use to draw a single conclusion. Finish by having students examine the Drawing Conclusions chart on the bottom of the page.

Extend the Handbook

Ask students to choose a character from a story or novel they've read recently. Have them use details from the work to create an inference equation for the character they've chosen.

Assessment

Ask students:

■ What does it mean to make an inference?

■ How can they use the thinking skill of drawing conclusions to get more from a text?

Comparing, Contrasting, and Evaluating

For use with *Reader's Handbook* page 48

Goals

In this lesson, students refine their understanding of two additional critical thinking skills: comparing and contrasting, and evaluating.

Teaching Focus

Background

Your students have been comparing, contrasting, and evaluating for years. In this lesson, you'll discuss what these critical thinking skills really are, in addition to how and why you use them. To make students' learning easier, make a link between these critical thinking skills and everyday life.

Instruction

Bring two pieces of fruit to class. Have students brainstorm a list of characteristics for each. Then explain that you want to *compare* (note similarities between) and *contrast* (note differences) the two kinds of fruit. Explain that students can use the thinking skill of comparing and contrasting while reading. For example, they might compare and contrast two characters, two settings, or two works as a whole. Then explain that any time students make judgments—for example, about books, clothes, or music—they are evaluating. Caution, however, that an evaluation must be carefully supported with facts and details for it to be valid.

Teaching Approach

Use of the Handbook

Direct students' attention to page 48. Read aloud the examples given and explain the idea that there are many different ways to examine how things are alike and different. Next, have students read silently the information on page 48 about evaluating. Ask students, When was the last time you found yourself evaluating something? What was the reason? Then explore with students how this critical thinking skill can help them become more effective readers.

Extend the Handbook

Ask students to complete pages 12–14 of *Student Applications Book 10.*

Assessment

Ask students:

■ Why is it helpful to compare and contrast when reading?

■ How can evaluating make you a stronger reader?

WEEK 3
Lesson 4 Reading Actively

For use with *Reader's Handbook* pages 49–52

Goals

In this lesson, students learn the importance of reading actively.

Teaching Focus

Background

Students who have trouble reading are often passive, rather than active, readers. Passive readers let an author's words crash over them, very much like waves on a beach. They assume that it's up to the author to convey everything they need to know. Active readers, on the other hand, take control of their reading. They use strategies to extract meaning instead of waiting for things to become clear to them. They question, clarify, react, and make connections to a work. Helping students become active readers is an important goal of the *Reader's Handbook*. In this lesson, you'll discuss what it means to be an "active" reader and how it can make a difference in students' reading abilities.

Instruction

Begin by asking students to share their reading "secrets." What kinds of habits and rituals do they follow that help them get the most out of a text? Then discuss the concept of reading actively. Explain the importance of taking notes while reading and holding a "conversation" with the author. Finish by exploring the six different ways a reader can annotate a text. Encourage students to practice each one.

Teaching Approach

Use of the Handbook

Have students follow along as you read the information on active reading on page 49. Be sure to point out the tips for active reading that appear in the middle of the page. Then have students read on their own the excerpt from *The Bonesetter's Daughter*. Encourage them to pay particular attention to the six ways a reader can annotate a passage. Finish the lesson with a group reading of pages 51–52. Help students spot the most important details on these two pages.

Extend the Handbook

Ask students to think about how active reading can help them get more from a textbook. How would they use these strategies with science or history, for example? Have students record their thoughts in their reading journals.

Assessment

Ask students:

- What are six ways of reading actively?

- What does it mean to stop and clarify what you're reading?

- What does it mean to react to a text?

WEEK 4
Lesson 1

Finding the Subject of a Paragraph

For use with *Reader's Handbook* pages 53–54

Goals

In this lesson, students explore the major characteristics of a paragraph and then focus on techniques for finding the subject.

Teaching Focus

Background

The paragraph is a basic unit of thought and contains even smaller units of thought, called *sentences*. Nonfiction writers tend to follow the same set of rules when structuring their paragraphs. (Fiction writers often bend the rules a bit.) The first rule nonfiction writers follow is that a paragraph must have a subject. The second is that it must have a main—or controlling—idea. The third is that it must contain three or more details in support of the main idea. A reader's first step when analyzing a paragraph is to find its subject. This is as easy as asking yourself, "What is the writer mostly talking about?"

Instruction

Open the unit with a general discussion of paragraphs. Explain that no reader stops to analyze every single paragraph in a text. However, it's important for readers to have a general understanding of how individual paragraphs contribute to the text as a whole. For this reason, you'll be spending this week on how to read, understand, and respond to a paragraph.

Teaching Approach

Use of the Handbook

Ask a volunteer to define the word *paragraph*. Then have other students chime in with the characteristics of a paragraph. Lead students to understand that every paragraph has a subject, a main idea (stated or implied), and a series of details that in some way support the main idea. Next, have students read the introduction to the chapter on page 53. Read aloud the instructions on finding the subject of a paragraph. Point out places a reader might look for clues about the subject.

Extend the Handbook

Gather sample paragraphs from various nonfiction texts, including textbooks, essays, news stories, and editorials. Ask each student to find one paragraph that they'd like to analyze. Have them read the paragraph and make notes about its subject.

Assessment

Ask students:

■ Why is it important for you to learn how to analyze a paragraph?

■ What question should you ask when thinking about the subject of a paragraph?

WEEK 4
Lesson 2
Finding the Main Idea

For use with *Reader's Handbook* pages 55–58

Goals

In this lesson, students learn how to identify the main idea of a paragraph.

Teaching Focus

Background

Identifying the main idea of a paragraph is an important test of students' ability to think inferentially. Here you'll spend a few minutes discussing stated main idea in a paragraph and then explore what readers need to do when the main idea is implied.

Instruction

Begin with a discussion of the difference between the subject of a paragraph and its main idea. Explain that the subject is what the author is mostly talking about, and the main idea is what the author is trying to tell the reader about the subject. To make your point, write the following main idea equation on the board:

Subject + what the author says about the subject = main idea

Use the handbook to help you explain the difference between stated and implied main idea.

Teaching Approach

Use of the Handbook

Direct students' attention to page 55 in the *Reader's Handbook*. Explain that an author may state the main idea in one of the sentences of the paragraph. More often, however, the author merely implies the main idea and expects the reader to figure out what he or she is trying to say. An example of this is the Gettysburg paragraph on page 54. The author never says that the Battle of Gettysburg was a pivotal one, but the implication is there. After pointing out this example, have students read the information on finding an implied main idea on page 56. See if they can identify the main idea of the paragraph from *Land of Promise*, and have them turn the page to see if their answer is correct. Point out the Main Idea Organizer on page 57 and mention that it is one of the most important tools in the handbook. Direct students to the page 747 of the Reading Tools section.

Extend the Handbook

For additional practice with finding the main idea, assign students pages 00–00 of *Student Applications Book 10*.

Assessment

Ask students:

■ What is the difference between a paragraph's subject and its main idea?

■ What formula can you use to find the main idea of a paragraph?

■ Why do authors tend to imply their main idea rather than state it directly?

WEEK 4
Lesson 3
Types of Paragraphs

For use with *Reader's Handbook* page 59

Goals

In this lesson, students explore four basic types of paragraphs and their purposes.

Teaching Focus

Background

In nonfiction writing, there are four basic types of paragraphs: narrative, persuasive, descriptive, and expository. (More sophisticated writing also may contain paragraphs of description and reflective paragraphs.) Each type serves a specific purpose, and the main idea of the paragraph will reflect that purpose. In this lesson, you'll explore each of the four types in some detail.

Instruction

Begin by explaining the purpose of the lesson: to learn about four basic types of paragraphs. Then divide the class into four groups. Assign one type of paragraph to each group. Direct group members to learn as much as they can about their type of paragraph and find at least one example in a textbook or newspaper article. Later, reconvene groups and ask a representative from each to report back to the class. End the lesson by having students read and then summarize the information on paragraphs in the *Reader's Handbook*.

Teaching Approach

Use of the Handbook

Direct students to refer to the handbook as needed. Have them read the relevant definition on page 59. After your whole-class discussion, ask students to read silently the information on page 59. Then work with students to complete a Magnet Summary for the word *paragraph*. (For more help with this tool, see page 747 in the Reading Tools section of the handbook.)

Extend the Handbook

Invite students to reflect upon the type of paragraph their group explored and then try their hand at writing one of their own. If students have trouble getting started, brainstorm possible topics for their paragraphs. One topic that would work for all four types of paragraphs would be "peer pressure."

Assessment

Ask students:

■ What are the four basic types of paragraphs?

■ How can you tell the difference between each?

■ How can understanding the type of paragraph you're reading improve your understanding of the text?

WEEK 4
Lesson 4

Ways of Organizing Paragraphs

For use with *Reader's Handbook* pages 60–69

Goals

Here students explore the most common ways of organizing the details in a paragraph.

Teaching Focus

Background

Writers are free to structure their paragraphs as they wish. In fact, some of the most brilliant modern writers seem determined to break conventional rules of paragraphing. Still, your students will benefit from a lesson on the most common ways of organizing details in a paragraph.

Instruction

Begin with a review of the three parts of a paragraph: subject, main idea, and supporting details. Then work with students to explore eight different ways of organizing the details in a paragraph: through time order, order of importance, cause-effect order, listing order, geographic order, comparison-contrast order, classification order, and mixed order. If you feel the list will overwhelm students, have groups reassemble in their groups from the previous lesson and assign two or more organizational types to each group. Ask group members to read about their paragraph types and then report to the class.

Teaching Approach

Use of the Handbook

Have students reread or skim pages 53–59 for review. Ask students, What are the three main components of a paragraph? Then launch a discussion of organizational types. Use pages 60–69 as support for your discussion.

Extend the Handbook

Once again, ask students to examine different texts and find one or more paragraphs that they'd like to analyze. Ask students to do an active reading of the paragraph they've selected and then make notes about how it is organized. See if students can make generalizations about the relationship between organization and purpose.

Assessment

Ask students:

■ What are some of the most common ways a paragraph can be structured?

■ Why is it important to identify the kind of paragraph you are reading?

WEEK 5
Reading History

For use with *Reader's Handbook* pages 73–87

Daily Lessons	Summary
Lesson 1 **Before Reading a** **History Text**	Discuss the chief characteristics of history textbooks and discuss how the reading process can help students get *more* from this type of text.
Lesson 2 **Asking *Who, What,*** ***Where, When, Why,*** **and *How* Questions**	Help students set a purpose for reading history by asking the 5 W's and H questions: *who, what, where, when, why,* and *how.*
Lesson 3 **Connecting to** **History Texts**	Explore how to make personal connections to the information contained in a history text.
Lesson 4 **Remembering** **History**	Work with students as they apply the After Reading stage of the reading process to a history text. Emphasize the importance of remembering key facts and details from each chapter.

Lesson Resources

Overheads
For this lesson, use:
Overheads 8 and 9: Previewing History

See *Student Applications Book 10* pages 20–30.

See *Test Book* for multiple-choice and short-answer tests.

See Website www.greatsource.com/rehand

For more practice, see also *Sourcebook* Grade 10, pages 33–48 and 197–218; *Daybook* Grade 10, pages 66–73.

WEEK 6

Reading Science

For use with *Reader's Handbook* pages 88–99

Daily Lessons	**Summary**
Lesson 1 **Before Reading a Science Text**	Discuss students' experience with science textbooks. Explore how the reading process can help them read and respond to this type of writing.
Lesson 2 **Reading with a Purpose**	Review the importance of setting a purpose and the types of purpose questions students might ask themselves before reading a science chapter.
Lesson 3 **Understanding Outlining**	Introduce the reading strategy of outlining and how students can use it with a science text.
Lesson 4 **After Reading a Science Text**	Ask students to apply what they know about the After Reading stage of the reading process to the sample science chapter in the *Reader's Handbook*.

Lesson Resources

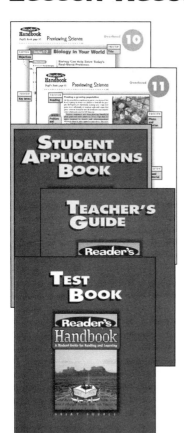

Overheads

For this lesson, use:

Overheads 10 and 11: Previewing Science

See *Student Applications Book 10* pages 31–39.

See *Teacher's Guide* pages 54–62.

See *Test Book* for multiple-choice and short-answer tests.

See Website www.greatsource.com/rehand

For more practice, see also
Sourcebook Grade 10, pages 220–238;
Daybook Grade 10, pages 55–57.

Before Reading a History Text

For use with *Reader's Handbook* pages 73–87

Goals

In this lesson, students become familiar with common characteristics of history textbooks and learn strategies for reading history.

Teaching Focus

Background

Students who approach their history textbooks with a sense of foreboding often think that historians are concerned only with the rote memorization of names, dates, places, and events. But historians are not merely interested in what happened and when. They also want to know *why* events happened and the ways in which people of the past have managed to change their lives—for better or worse. This lesson makes the world of the past more accessible to students by explaining how history textbooks are organized and by equipping students with several approaches for connecting with and assimilating historical information.

Instruction

Familiarize students with common features of history textbooks, such as maps and timelines, and the concepts of chronological and geographical order. Ask volunteers to discuss why history textbooks include these elements. Then have students describe how they might use the Before Reading stage of the reading process to tackle a history assignment.

Teaching Approach

Use of the Handbook

Divide students into small groups. Refer them to page 83 of the *Reader's Handbook* and ask them to look at the passage showing examples of chronological and geographical order. Then have them turn to page 75 and identify instances of chronological and geographical order in "Deserts, Towns, and Travelers."

Extend the Handbook

Ask students to turn to a chapter in their history textbooks. Have them practice identifying elements of history texts and explaining their purpose.

Assessment

Ask students:

■ What are two common ways that material is organized in history textbooks?

■ How can maps, timelines, and graphic material help you understand historical information?

Asking *Who, What, Where, When, Why,* and *How* Questions

For use with *Reader's Handbook* pages 74–82

Goals

In this lesson, students learn how the 5 W's and H can provide a framework for reading history textbooks.

Teaching Focus

Background

Asking the 5 W's and H—*who, what, where, when, why,* and *how*—is a simple but highly effective way for students to establish a purpose for their reading and determine a focus for their note-taking. Explain to students that asking these questions throughout the reading helps to sustain their interest in the subject and to deepen their understanding. Show them how they can use two note-taking styles—Reporter's Notes and Key Word or Topic Notes—for history texts.

Instruction

Have volunteers imagine they are newspaper reporters who have traveled to Medina to write a profile on Muhammad. Have students list the questions they would ask Muhammad. Write the questions on the board in the style of Reporter's Notes. Lead students to see that the reporter's 5 W's and H are also useful for studying history.

Teaching Approach

Use of the Handbook

Have a volunteer read Set a Purpose on page 74 of the handbook. Then form small groups and have students work through pages 74–81. Visit each group to make sure that they understand the process of setting a purpose, previewing, and planning.

Extend the Handbook

Have students choose a chapter from their history textbooks to practice the Before Reading steps of setting a purpose, planning, and previewing.

Assessment

Ask students:

■ How can answering the 5 W's and H clarify your purpose for reading history?

■ How can the Before Reading steps and strategy of note-taking make you a more active reader?

WEEK 5
Lesson 3
Connecting to History Texts

For use with *Reader's Handbook* page 84

Goals

This lesson impresses upon students the value of making personal connections to history.

Teaching Focus

Background

The study of history can help students understand today's culture by acquainting them with the experience of people in other times and places. It also can sharpen students' analytical skills and train them for a lifetime of critical thinking. You can help students forge connections to what they learn in history texts by teaching them how to remain actively engaged as they read and how to connect the people and events in history to their own lives.

Instruction

Provide a model for the students by revealing your own reactions to a person or event discussed in their history textbooks. Describe the questions you asked yourself as you read and the details that helped you arrive at your impressions. Then ask volunteers to propose other questions that they might ask themselves as they read history texts. List their responses on the board.

Teaching Approach

Use of the Handbook

Ask a volunteer to read aloud the first two paragraphs on page 84. Then ask students to read "The Rise of Islam," beginning on page 75 in the handbook, and jot down their questions and reflections. Invite students to share their thoughts with the class. To help them connect to the text, suggest that they create a Making Connections Chart (see page 748).

Extend the Handbook

For additional practice, have students repeat the exercise using a reading in their history textbooks. Encourage students to reflect in their journals on the process of connecting to history.

Assessment

Ask students:

■ How does making a personal connection affect your understanding and memory of historical information?

■ How can making connections help make history relevant to you?

WEEK 5
Lesson 4

Remembering History

For use with *Reader's Handbook* pages 84–87

Goals

Here students will learn strategies for remembering historical facts and assessing their significance.

Teaching Focus

Background

In the three previous lessons, students learned the importance of actively reading history. Students will now discover how well their engagement with the material can pay off as they begin memorizing what they've learned. Reviewing, rereading, and augmenting their notes will make it easier for students to master history assignments.

Instruction

Begin by asking students to describe what they typically do after they finish reading a history chapter. Point out the value of pausing and reflecting upon what they've read. Then suggest that they peruse the material in the handbook again to gain a clearer understanding of the information offered and to fill in gaps in their notes. Encourage them either to create a graphic organizer or add to their notes to further reinforce what they've read. Emphasize the value of using their notes as a way to remember the material.

Teaching Approach

Use of the Handbook

Have students read the After Reading steps listed on pages 84–87. Then have students return to page 86 to discuss the graphic organizer. Ask them how such an organizer might help them make notes and memorize the highlights of a history chapter. Point out that the process of manipulating the material can help them retain a surprising amount of what they've read. Next, discuss how doing research and conducting an interview can help students remember the material. Ask volunteers to suggest other ideas for remembering.

Extend the Handbook

Ask students to pair up. Have them list search terms that they might use to research Islam on the Internet. Then ask them to write a list of interview questions about Islam that will help them commit the material to memory.

Assessment

Ask students:

■ What strategies help you remember historical information best?

■ What are some ways you can remember what you've read better?

WEEK 6
Lesson 1

Before Reading a Science Text

For use with *Reader's Handbook* pages 88–93

Goals

In this lesson, students learn how to read science texts effectively.

Teaching Focus

Background

While some students understand science intuitively, others find biology, physics, and other scientific topics daunting. The terminology alone is often so complex that many students despair of ever comprehending it. But the reading and study strategies in this lesson can help demystify science.

Instruction

Ask students to discuss their previous experience with science textbooks and to brainstorm the common features of these texts. Which elements do they find helpful? What aspects of reading science do they find difficult? Then briefly review the three steps of the Before Reading stage of the reading process. Explain the benefits of using these steps when reading a science textbook. Work with students as they preview the sample science chapter in the *Reader's Handbook*.

Teaching Approach

Use of the Handbook

Ask students to read the description of the Before Reading process on pages 88–89. Discuss the three steps and how they can help students overcome the challenges of reading science. Then have students refer to pages 90–93 and practice the Preview process. Invite them to make notes in their reading journals.

Extend the Handbook

Ask students to practice the Preview process using the first chapter of their science textbooks. Suggest that they write comments on sticky notes. Then come together as a class to discuss what they were able to glean from their preview of the chapter. Ask volunteers to comment on the effect their preview might have on their careful reading of the text.

For additional practice, have students complete pages 31–39 in *Student Applications Book 10*.

Assessment

Ask students:

■ How can Before Reading strategies help you get more from a science text?

■ In what ways has this lesson changed your view of reading science?

WEEK 6
Lesson 2

Reading with a Purpose

For use with *Reader's Handbook* pages 89–93

Goals

In this lesson, students discover the importance of reading science slowly and methodically—in much the same way that a scientist goes about working through an experiment.

Teaching Focus

Background

Just as scientists carry out experiments in a systematic way, students can improve their understanding of science if they read it with a clear purpose—or set of purpose questions—in mind. This section teaches students the tools and strategies they can use while reading a science text. In addition, students will explore the typical organization of a science text and how many science concepts hinge upon classification, cause and effect, and problem-solution.

Instruction

Have students recall the process of setting a purpose. List their purpose questions on the board. Then ask students to read carefully the sample science chapter, keeping their purpose questions in mind as they read. After they finish reading, discuss how a reader's purpose might change during a reading. Explain that modifying their reading purpose as needed is something proficient readers do automatically as they read. Finish the lesson with instruction on how science textbooks are organized and three types of organization students will see most often in their science texts.

Teaching Approach

Use of the Handbook

Have a student volunteer read aloud the information on outlining on the bottom of page 94 of the handbook. Review the sample outline on this page and on the page that follows. Discuss Topic Outlines versus Sentence Outlines and the advantages and disadvantages of each. Then explore how outlines can help students organize the information in a science textbook.

Extend the Handbook

Ask students to turn to a chapter in their science textbooks. Have them set a purpose using the three suggestions described in the handbook. Ask volunteers to share their statements of purpose. Encourage students to reflect on the process in their journals.

Assessment

Ask students:

■ What does it mean to "read with a purpose"?

■ How are most science textbooks organized?

WEEK 6
Lesson 3
Understanding Outlining

For use with *Reader's Handbook* pages 94–96

Goals

This lesson teaches students the strategy of outlining and the effect the strategy can have on a reader's comprehension of a science text.

Teaching Focus

Background

The strategy of outlining can facilitate students' mastery of science in several different ways. First, the process of creating an outline can be a helpful exercise in discriminating between important and unimportant details. Second, outlining can help students see how one set of details relates to the next. This is a necessary lesson, since many science concepts hinge one upon the other. In addition, the act of creating the outline can make essential details easier to recall for a homework assignment, an experiment, or a test.

Instruction

Ask volunteers to describe their previous experience with outlining. Have students explain the benefits of this strategy. Then begin your direct instruction of the strategy.

Teaching Approach

Use of the Handbook

Ask students to read pages 94–96 in the handbook. Outlining might seem confusing to some students, so allow plenty of time for questions after they finish reading. Then have students copy in their reading journals the outline shown on page 95. Ask them to make notes on this outline during their careful reading of the science chapter.

If students need additional help with the strategy, have them read pages 720–721 in the Strategy Handbook.

Extend the Handbook

Have students create two preliminary outlines for a chapter from their own science textbooks—one formal and one informal. Remind them to use the headings from the chapter and to leave plenty of room for their during-reading notes.

Assessment

Ask students:

■ How can outlining strengthen your understanding of scientific material?

■ How does outlining differ from other note-taking strategies?

WEEK 6
Lesson 4

After Reading a Science Text

For use with *Reader's Handbook* pages 90–93, 97–99

Goals

Here students focus on steps to take after reading scientific material.

Teaching Focus

Background

One reason that many students resist reading science is that they do not immediately grasp the individual concepts or understand how these concepts relate to their own lives. What they don't realize, of course, is that very few people fully absorb scientific information after a single reading. By following the After Reading steps presented in the *Reader's Handbook,* students can become more confident about their ability to process what they've read.

Instruction

Begin by reassuring students that even accomplished scientists struggle to understand difficult concepts. Ask them to brainstorm the After Reading strategies they've read about thus far. Which ones would be most useful in understanding a science chapter? Remind them that outlines and graphic organizers make excellent study aids.

Teaching Approach

Use of the Handbook

Have students read the After Reading steps listed on pages 97–99. Emphasize the importance of connecting to what they've read. Then ask students to turn to pages 92–93, "Biology Can Help Fight Diseases." Divide students into small groups and have them apply the After Reading steps to this part of the chapter. Stress the importance of pausing and reflecting and rereading. Provide students with index cards for creating Study Cards.

Extend the Handbook

Have students remain in their small groups and work through the activities for remembering science. Ask each group to choose one topic for further research and describe what resources they would consult for information. Then have group members write practice test questions for the science chapter they have just read.

Assessment

Ask students:

■ How can the strategy of outlining help you memorize scientific information?

■ In what ways can the strategy of note-taking help you understand science material?

WEEK 7
Reading Math

For use with *Reader's Handbook* pages 100–111

Daily Lessons	Summary
Lesson 1 **Before Reading a Math Text**	Discuss the three steps of the Before Reading stage of the reading process and how they work with a math textbook.
Lesson 2 **Visualizing and Thinking Aloud**	Model using the strategy of visualizing and thinking aloud. Explore the ways in which it can help students solve more challenging math problems.
Lesson 3 **How Math Texts Are Organized**	Review with students the structure and features of a math text.
Lesson 4 **After Reading a Math Text**	Introduce after Reading strategies students can use to help them remember math material.

Lesson Resources

Overheads

For this lesson, use:

Overheads 12 and 13: Previewing Math

See *Student Applications Book 10* pages 40–46.

See *Teacher's Guide* pages 63–70.

See *Test Book* for multiple-choice and short-answer tests.

See Website www.greatsource.com/rehand

Elements of Textbooks

For use with *Reader's Handbook* pages 134–151

Daily Lessons	Summary
Lesson 1 **Using Elements of Textbooks**	Explore the purpose of and how to use the *Reader's Handbook* Elements of Textbooks section.
Lesson 2 **Standard Textbook Features**	Discuss how textbooks are often organized and describe such standard features as study guide boxes, boldface terms, section headings, and end-of-chapter questions.
Lesson 3 **Textbook Graphics**	Help students realize how reading the graphics in a textbook chapter can strengthen their understanding of the written material.
Lesson 4 **Front and Back Matter in a Textbook**	Discuss the purposes for a textbook's front matter and back matter. Activate students' prior knowledge of how to use these features.

Lesson Resources

See *Teacher's Guide* pages 88–101.

See *Test Book* for multiple-choice and short-answer tests.

See *Content Area Guide: Social Studies* and *Content Area Guide: Science.*

See Website www.greatsource.com/rehand

WEEK 7
Lesson 1
Before Reading a Math Text

For use with *Reader's Handbook* pages 100–104

Goals

In this lesson, students learn techniques for applying Before Reading strategies to a math text.

Teaching Focus

Background

The pages of math textbooks abound with numbers and symbols. However, the key to understanding mathematical concepts, operations, and relationships rests in reading the explanatory text that accompanies the equations. This lesson impresses upon students the importance of reading math texts just as attentively as they read a story or poem. Ultimately, students can gain not only a solid grounding in math but also excellent problem-solving skills that they can use in other areas of study.

Instruction

Ask students to describe the ideal conditions for studying math. Lead them to realize the advantage of being focused and alert. Then have students discuss how they would apply the Before Reading steps to a math chapter. Ask them to compare and contrast the process of reading a math text with reading other subjects. Help them to discover how titles, boldface words, and other textbook elements can be just as useful for setting a purpose in math as they are for other subjects. A Preview is a valuable first step for reading a math text.

Teaching Approach

Use of the Handbook

Have students read pages 100–101 of the *Reader's Handbook*. Then ask them to preview the sample chapter on pages 102–104. Discuss what they learned from previewing the text. Ask them how they can use the Preview step to set a purpose for reading. Then divide the students into three groups and have them work together to write several purpose questions for their reading of the sample chapter.

Extend the Handbook

To reinforce the importance of the Before Reading stage, have students preview a chapter in their math textbooks. Ask them to make preview notes on an organizer, such as a Web or Magnet Summary.

Assessment

Ask students:

- In what ways is reading a math text similar to reading a history text?

- How can the Before Reading stage help you in reading math?

WEEK 7
Lesson 2

Visualizing and Thinking Aloud

For use with *Reader's Handbook* pages 103, 105–106

Goals

Here students learn how the strategy of visualizing and thinking aloud can help them make sense of complicated math problems.

Teaching Focus

Background

Drawings and musings—whether on paper, in one's mind, or out loud—can simplify abstract ideas and complex word problems. In this lesson, you can validate doodling in the margins and talking through problems as a superb way to read math. Students can best learn the strategy of visualizing and thinking aloud by having you model it for them and then practicing the process themselves.

Instruction

Choose a simple word problem from the students' math textbook or think of a problem from your daily life that you can solve with math. As you describe the problem to students, sketch a drawing on the board and model the process of thinking aloud. Ask students to suggest other strategies they might use to solve the problem. Point out that, rather than thinking aloud, you might have created a list of steps for solving it.

Teaching Approach

Use of the Handbook

Have students read independently pages 105–106 of the handbook. Then divide the class into small groups and ask them to illustrate the four basic number operations found on page 103. Before they begin, reiterate that their sketches don't need to be perfect or even particularly detailed. What's important is that students create a drawing that can help them solve the mathematical problem.

Extend the Handbook

Have students choose a word problem from their math textbooks. Have them copy the problem in their reading journals and then solve it using the strategy of visualizing and thinking aloud. As a class, discuss the helpfulness of the strategy with this type of problem.

Assessment

Ask students:

■ Why is it important to visualize a math problem? How can the process of visualizing help you solve the problem?

■ In what instances would it be helpful to use the strategy of visualizing and thinking aloud?

WEEK 7
Lesson 3

How Math Texts Are Organized

For use with *Reader's Handbook* pages 108–109

Goals

In this lesson, students learn how understanding the structure of a math text can help them more easily find key details in each chapter.

Teaching Focus

Background

Math texts reflect the nature of mathematics itself. They follow a logical format that is meant to help students learn basic to advanced mathematical concepts and operations. This lesson acquaints students with common features and organization of math texts.

Instruction

Explain that math textbooks are divided into chapters, which are then subdivided into sections. Discuss the four major features of a math lesson: the opening explanation, sample problems, graphs and diagrams, and exercises. Ask volunteers to tell how they would use these four features to help them read. Lead students to see that knowledge of the organization of the lessons helps focus their reading purpose throughout the lesson

Teaching Approach

Use of the Handbook

Have students read page 108. Then have them turn to the sample algebra chapter on pages 102–104. Ask them to locate and identify the four organizational elements. Discuss how all four parts of math chapters complement and reinforce each other. Then ask students to imagine if the sample chapter did not include the opening explanation. How would this affect their comprehension of the chapter? Stress that it is essential to read the opening explanation carefully and deliberately.

Extend the Handbook

Have students turn to the same chapter of their math text that they used previously and use sticky notes to identify key organizational features. Then explain the different purposes of each section. Point out the strategy of close reading for use with the opening paragraph and that the strategies of note-taking and visualizing and thinking aloud will work well with the remaining sections.

Assessment

Ask students:

■ What purpose does each part of a math lesson serve?

■ What strategies are helpful in reading math?

WEEK 7
Lesson 4
After Reading a Math Text

For use with *Reader's Handbook* pages 108–111

Goals

Here students learn what to do after reading that can maximize their understanding of math material.

Teaching Focus

Background

The After Reading stage of the reading process is crucial with math because it affords students an opportunity to master key concepts and become adept at solving the types of problems presented in each chapter. In this lesson, you'll expose students to the need for reinforcing what they've read. It is important that students appreciate the usefulness of this rereading stage. Students can easily forget what they've read if they don't review the material and put it to use in homework assignments.

Instruction

Ask volunteers to recall the three components of the After Reading stage. Have them explore how they would use these steps to help them remember math material. Explain that note-taking is a particularly useful rereading strategy because it reinforces the material and creates a study tool that students can use later.

Teaching Approach

Use of the Handbook

Have students turn to page 109 in the handbook and read the questions listed under Looking Back. Ask them to answer the questions in their journals to assess their understanding of the sample chapter. Then invite students to reflect on what steps they would take to improve their understanding of the chapter. Emphasize the value of note-taking, forming study groups, and creating practice tests.

Extend the Handbook

Ask students to return to the chapter they've been consulting in their math text. Have them assess their understanding of a chapter by answering the Looking Back questions. Ask them to use note-taking to improve their comprehension of the material. Have students pair up and write a few practice test questions.

For additional practice, have students complete pages 40–46 in *Student Applications Book 10*.

Assessment

Ask students:

■ What strategies can you use after reading a math chapter to help you better understand the material?

■ Why is note-taking an important After Reading strategy to use with math?

WEEK 8
Lesson 1

Using Elements of Textbooks

For use with *Reader's Handbook* pages 134–151

Goals

In this lesson, students learn how to get the most out of the *Reader's Handbook's* Elements of Textbooks section.

Teaching Focus

Background

Textbook editors and writers gather information that is scattered throughout thousands of books and monographs about a subject and synthesize it into one book. Students who don't have an understanding of how textbooks are organized can feel overwhelmed by the barrage of information. This lesson teaches them to use the Elements of Textbooks unit as a reference guide.

Instruction

Ask students to imagine that they work for a major publisher of educational books. Their assignment is to write a social studies textbook for tenth graders. Have students identify the elements that they would include based on their previous experience with reading textbooks. As students name different elements, write them on the board and ask students to discuss how each one facilitates learning. Then have students write a journal entry about reading textbooks. Have them address which elements they find helpful and which tend to be confusing or hard to use.

Teaching Approach

Use of the Handbook

Have a volunteer read aloud page 134 of the *Reader's Handbook*. Then ask students to preview the Elements of Textbooks section on pages 134–151. Have them jot down notes about what stands out as most important to them.

Extend the Handbook

Ask students to select one of the textbooks they're using and have them preview one chapter. Have them to make notes listing all of the elements found in their textbook.

Assessment

Ask students:

■ What are some key elements of textbooks?

■ In what ways can the Elements of Textbooks in the *Reader's Handbook* help you read your textbooks more effectively?

WEEK 8
Lesson 2

Standard Textbook Features

For use with *Reader's Handbook* pages 135, 145, 149–151

Goals

In this lesson, students become more acquainted with common textbook features and learn how these features can enhance their studies.

Teaching Focus

Background

Standard textbook features such as typography and headings are meant to focus students' attention on the most salient information in the book. In addition, they make the presentation of subject matter more orderly and understandable. Building on students' prior exposure to textbooks, this lesson will reinforce how textbook elements help students read effectively and enhance comprehension.

Instruction

Explain to students that this lesson covers features that give textbook chapters a clear structure. Ask volunteers to brainstorm the purpose of chapter preview boxes and study questions. Write their thoughts on the board. After forming small groups, have students read the description of chapter previews on page 135 and the explanation of study questions and reviews on page 145. Ask students, How are previews and study questions similar? In what ways are they different?

Teaching Approach

Use of the Handbook

Walk students through the discussion of typography and headings on pages 149–151. Ask volunteers to explain the difference between boldface and italic type. Then discuss the purpose of headings. Emphasize that the six common types of headings in a chapter give structure to textbooks. Have students imagine that the sample textbook page on page 150 did not include any headings. Ask students, Would you be able to figure out the subject of the chapter and how the information is organized? Guide students to see how headings can bolster reading comprehension.

Extend the Handbook

Have students thumb through a chapter in one of their textbooks, focus on its major organizational features, and write a journal entry about what they noticed.

Assessment

Ask students:

■ How can standard features help you read a textbook?

■ Which textbook features do you find most helpful? Why?

WEEK 8
Lesson 3

Textbook Graphics

For use with *Reader's Handbook* pages 136–137, 141–144, 148

Goals

In this lesson, students learn that interpreting graphics can improve their understanding of textbook material.

Teaching Focus

Background

Students will often merely glance over charts, graphs, maps, photos, and timelines and then dismiss them as simply aesthetic. Perhaps they consider these graphics a distraction from the text. In this lesson, you can convince students that graphics matter. Graphics demonstrate material in an efficient manner and afford students a quick reference tool for reading and reviewing. Here students will become familiar with the purpose of various types of graphics and learn how to read them.

Instruction

Ask students to brainstorm the types of graphics they might expect to find in a textbook. Write their responses on the board. The list should include charts, tables, fine art, and even cartoons. Explain that graphics have two important functions: they make textbooks easier to read by interrupting running text, and they help students visualize concepts and reinforce ideas discussed in the chapter.

Teaching Approach

Use of the Handbook

Walk students through pages 136–137. Describe charts and the various types of graphics, including pie, bar, and line graphs. Reinforce the efficacy of turning the title of a chart or graph into a question. Call students' attention to how one student took notes on a graph on page 137. Then proceed to pages 141–144. First, describe the features of maps and model how students should read them. Encourage students to describe in their own words what the map shows. Second, explain to students that photos, illustrations, and captions can provide an instant snapshot of a chapter's content. Third, define the four special features of a textbook and discuss how students can use them. Fourth, lead students to see that timelines can help them visualize a sequence of events.

Extend the Handbook

Have students read the map on page 141 of the handbook. Ask them to write a paragraph that puts into their own words what the map is depicting.

Assessment

Ask students:

■ What is one kind of textbook graphic and what is its purpose?

■ What are two reasons textbooks include graphics?

WEEK 8
Lesson 4

Front and Back Matter in a Textbook

For use with *Reader's Handbook* pages 138–140, 146–147

Goals

Here students will learn that front and back matter can help them navigate a textbook and review for exams.

Teaching Focus

Background

Even the most proficient readers sometimes neglect to use the front and back matter (the table of contents, indexes, glossaries, endnotes, and so on) in a textbook. Tucked in the outermost reaches of textbooks, these pages are easy to overlook. Aside from consulting the table of contents when they've forgotten to mark their place, readers rarely take full advantage of these undervalued study tools. In this lesson, students learn how to get the most out of front and back matter.

Instruction

List the terms *table of contents, index, glossary,* and *endnotes* on the board. Ask students to explain the function of each. After helping them arrive at precise definitions, explain that all of these features can be used as learning tools. Ask volunteers to brainstorm instances in which each type of front and back matter can help them review for an exam.

Teaching Approach

Use of the Handbook

Have students read pages 146–147. Reinforce the two uses for the table of contents. Suggest that students adopt the idea of making a study guide by copying the table of contents into their notebook and leaving room for their own notes about a chapter. Then ask students to read about footnotes, indexes, and glossaries on pages 138–140. Stress that indexes and glossaries can help them study for exams efficiently by making terms and definitions easily accessible.

Extend the Handbook

Ask students to write a short journal entry describing how they would use various types of front and back matter during each stage of the reading process. Ask students to discuss which features are most useful Before, During, and After Reading.

Assessment

Ask students:

■ How can you use a table of contents to help you understand a chapter you are reading?

■ What is a glossary and how can you use it to help you study?

WEEK 9
Reading a Personal Essay

For use with *Reader's Handbook* pages 155–167

Daily Lessons	Summary
Lesson 1 **Understanding Essays**	Review general characteristics of personal essays and contrast them with the characteristics of expository essays. Activate prior knowledge about essays students have read in the past.
Lesson 2 **Before Reading a Personal Essay**	Discuss with students Before Reading strategies appropriate for reading a personal essay.
Lesson 3 **Reading a Personal Essay**	Help students complete a successful active reading of a personal essay.
Lesson 4 **After Reading a Personal Essay**	Review the three steps of the After Reading stage of the reading process. Explore strategies that work well with personal essays.

Lesson Resources

Overheads
For this lesson, use:
Overheads 14 and 15: Previewing a Personal Essay

See *Student Applications Book 10* pages 57–64.

See *Teacher's Guide* pages 103–110.

See *Test Book* for multiple-choice and short-answer tests.

See Website www.greatsource.com/rehand

For more practice, see also
Sourcebook Grade 10, pages 124–133;
Daybook Grade 10, pages 46–47, 58–60.

WEEK 10
Reading a Memoir

For use with *Reader's Handbook* pages 210–224

Daily Lessons	Summary
Lesson 1 **Understanding Memoirs**	Discuss characteristics of memoirs and what distinguishes them from other nonfiction writing.
Lesson 2 **Before Reading a Memoir**	Explore the steps of the Before Reading stage of the reading process and how to use them with a memoir. Provide an introduction to the strategy of synthesizing.
Lesson 3 **Reading a Memoir**	Support students as they complete an active reading of an excerpt from *Out of Africa*.
Lesson 4 **After Reading a Memoir**	Refine students' understanding of the After Reading stage of the reading process. Discuss its application to a memoir.

Lesson Resources

Overheads
For this lesson, use:
Overheads 22 and 23: Previewing a Memoir

See *Student Applications Book 10* pages 94–104.

See *Teacher's Guide* pages 140–149.

See *Test Book* for multiple-choice and short-answer tests.

See Website www.greatsource.com/rehand

For more practice, see also
Sourcebook Grade 10, pages 41–50, 52–63, 74–81, 161–178; *Daybook* Grade 10, pages 53, 58–60.

WEEK 9
Lesson 1 Understanding Essays

For use with *Reader's Handbook* pages 154–167

Goals

In this lesson, students learn the characteristics of personal essays and activate prior knowledge of the genre.

Teaching Focus

Background

There are two major types of nonfiction: expository and narrative. Expository nonfiction is factual and informative writing—the kind students read in their school textbooks. Narrative nonfiction tells a true story about an interesting person or event. Personal essays are a form of narrative nonfiction. Characteristics of a personal essay include possible use of the first person, a relatively informal or conversational tone, and an attempt by the author to reflect on what he or she has described.

Instruction

Open with a discussion of the different types of nonfiction in general and characteristics of personal essays in particular. Help students understand that a personal essay is a more informal kind of nonfiction writing and that some personal essays are written in the first person. Ask students to brainstorm examples of personal essays they've read in the past. Then explain that over the course of the week they will analyze a personal essay written by award-winning contemporary author N. Scott Momaday.

Teaching Approach

Use of the Handbook

Ask a volunteer to read aloud page 154. Ask another student to summarize the information on the page. Then direct students' attention to page 155. Discuss the handbook's definition of an essay and the three goals listed in the Goals box. Finish by asking students to preview pages 156–167.

Extend the Handbook

Ask students to reflect upon this introductory lesson in their reading journals. Have them make notes about key terms and ideas and then consider the ways in which the reading process might work with a personal essay. When they've finished, have volunteers share what they've written with the class.

Assessment

Ask students:

■ What is a personal essay and how is it different from an expository essay?

■ What did you learn about essays from previewing this section of the handbook?

WEEK 9
Lesson 2
Before Reading a Personal Essay

For use with *Reader's Handbook* pages 156, 726–727

Goals

In this lesson, students learn to apply the three steps of the Before Reading stage of the reading process to a personal essay.

Teaching Focus

Background

You'll want to give students some basic information about essay structure before they read Momaday's essay. Explain to students that an essay has three main parts: the introduction, body, and conclusion. Within one of these parts is the author's thesis statement, or main idea. The main idea is the big idea the author is trying to express. In a personal essay, the main idea often concerns a lesson the author has learned.

Instruction

After your discussion of the three parts of an essay, work with students to apply the three stages of the reading process to essays. Then direct students' attention to the Before Reading stage. Ask a volunteer to summarize the three steps of this stage and the purpose of each one. Then begin your discussion of how to apply the three steps to a personal essay, emphasizing the importance of the Preview stage.

Teaching Approach

Use of the Handbook

Ask a volunteer to read aloud pages 726–727 in the Strategy Handbook. Explain that part of their purpose when reading a personal essay is to make inferences about the author's main idea. Then direct students to page 156. Read aloud the information on setting a purpose and previewing an essay. Then work with students to preview Momaday's essay. If students are having trouble, "think aloud" as you work your way through the Preview Checklist.

Extend the Handbook

Gather several examples of essays and invite students to preview one. Ask them to duplicate the Preview Checklist from page 156 in their reading journals and then make notes about their essay on the checklist.

Assessment

Ask students:

■ What is your purpose for reading an essay?

■ What kinds of things should you look for when previewing an essay?

■ How does previewing an essay help you read more actively?

WEEK 9 **Reading a Personal Essay**

For use with *Reader's Handbook* pages 157–162, 251

Goals

In this lesson, students apply the During Reading stage of the reading process to a personal essay.

Teaching Focus

Background

Understanding the main idea of an essay requires some knowledge of how to interpret the author's purpose. Most essayists are said to have one or more of these purposes in mind when writing: to entertain, to persuade, to enlighten or teach, or to reveal a universal truth. Good readers often pick up on purpose clues (such as word choice) at the Preview stage.

Instruction

Open the lesson with a discussion of author's purpose. Use page 251 of the Elements of Nonfiction section of the *Reader's Handbook* to support what you say. Then teach students the strategy of outlining. Have them read the information on page 159 and then reinforce the idea that outlining can help a reader separate important from unimportant details in an essay. Then have students do a careful reading of Momaday's essay. Finish with a discussion of the importance of making a personal connection to the writing.

Teaching Approach

Use of the Handbook

Have a student volunteer read aloud the information at the bottom of page 158. Ask another volunteer to read aloud page 159 on using the strategy of outlining. Walk students through the information and sample student Outline on pages 161–162. Then ask students to do a careful reading of Momaday's essay and make notes on an Outline they've created in their journals.

Extend the Handbook

Have students return to the essay they previewed in the previous lesson and read it carefully. Reinforce students' understanding of outlining by asking them to outline this essay as well. Have students who need additional practice with the strategy complete pages 57–64 of *Student Applications Book 10*.

Assessment

Ask students:

■ Why is outlining a good reading strategy for an essay?

■ Why is it important to separate important from unimportant details in an essay?

WEEK 9
Lesson 4

After Reading a Personal Essay

For use with *Reader's Handbook* pages 164–167

Goals

Here students learn strategies for interpreting the main idea of an essay and reflecting upon and then evaluating the message the essayist has for readers.

Teaching Focus

Background

An important part of reading actively is making inferences—reasonable guesses—about the author's message and then evaluating the validity of that message and its applications to the reader's own life. Proficient readers rely on After Reading steps to ensure that they can understand and evaluate the information in an essay.

Instruction

Explain that in this lesson you'll discuss how to interpret and then evaluate an essayist's message. Begin by reviewing the steps of the After Reading stage of the reading process. Reinforce the importance of pausing and reflecting after a first reading. Model the kinds of questions good readers ask themselves at this point, such as "What is the author's message in this essay?", "Is the message well supported?", "What are my feelings about the message?", or "Has this essay in some way changed my view of the world?" Then discuss the rereading strategy of questioning the author. Explain the purpose of the strategy and how it might be used with a personal essay.

Teaching Approach

Use of the Handbook

Have students reread the information on connecting to a personal essay (page 164) if you feel they need the review. Then have students work in small groups to apply the After Reading strategies discussed on pages 164–167 to Momaday's essay. Help students develop their own Looking Back questions and encourage groups to spend time discussing the answers.

Extend the Handbook

Ask students to create a Main Idea Organizer for an essay and check to be sure they can restate the main idea and supporting details in the work. If there's time, have them write a short evaluation of the essay as a whole.

Assessment

Ask students:

■ How do you find the main idea of an essay?

■ What should you do after you find an essay's main idea and supporting details?

WEEK 10
Lesson 1   Understanding Memoirs

For use with *Reader's Handbook* page 210

Goals

In this lesson, students explore the genre of memoir and discuss how it compares to other types of nonfiction.

Teaching Focus

Background

A memoir is a personal narrative that focuses on a specific period in the author's life and describes in some detail the persons, events, or times known to author. It differs from an autobiography in that it provides a detailed snapshot of a certain time in the writer's life, rather than an account of the writer's entire life. Another difference between a memoir and an autobiography is that memoirists are usually persons who have played roles in, or have been close observers of, historical events. The memoirist takes it upon himself or herself to describe those events in some detail while at the same time reflecting upon their influence and effects.

Instruction

Begin by explaining that the purpose of this lesson is to discuss the characteristics of a memoir. Ask students, What does the word *memoir* make you think about? What exactly is a memoir? As a class, discuss characteristics of the genre and how it differs from a biography and an autobiography. Invite volunteers to name memoirs they've read or heard about. Then introduce Isak Dinesen's *Out of Africa*. Some of your students may have read the book or seen the movie. If so, ask one of them to summarize Dinesen's story.

Teaching Approach

Use of the Handbook

After your discussion of the characteristics of a memoir, ask students to turn to the *Reader's Handbook* and read the opening paragraph on page 210. Point out the final sentence of the first paragraph. Be sure students understand that a memoirist often focuses on the part of his or her life that affected him or her most significantly. Explain that one purpose for reading a memoir is to discover what effect the events and ideas of the time had on the writer.

Extend the Handbook

Ask each group to borrow a copy of *Out of Africa* from the library. Assign chapters from the book for students to read. As an initial activity, have students preview the chapter they've been assigned to read, making preview notes as they go.

Assessment

Ask students:

■ What is a memoir?

■ How is it different from other types of nonfiction? How is it the same?

WEEK 10
Lesson 2
Before Reading a Memoir

For use with *Reader's Handbook* pages 210–215

Goals

This lesson explains what to do before reading a memoir.

Teaching Focus

Background

A memoirist writes with two general purposes in mind: to tell a compelling story of a part of his or her life, and to tell about the people, places, and times that had an influence on his or her personality. The reader's purpose is to understand all that the author describes. In addition, a reader will expect to derive some enjoyment from the writing and perhaps learn something about himself or herself.

Instruction

Explain that in this lesson you'll be discussing both author's and reader's purpose, as well as what students should look for at the Preview stage of reading a memoir. In addition, you'll introduce the strategy of synthesizing and explain its uses with nonfiction. Later, students will learn the strategy's applications to fiction.

Teaching Approach

Use of the Handbook

Have students read silently the Before Reading information on pages 210 and 211. Then ask them to preview *Out of Africa*. Remind readers that the best way to preview a longer work is to look at the front and back covers and the table of contents, where appropriate. After they finish previewing, read aloud the information under Plan (page 214). Discuss the strategy of synthesizing and explain how it can help students get more from a work of nonfiction. Point out the six general topics readers can expect to find in a memoir. Finish by asking students to generate their own purpose questions for *Out of Africa*.

Extend the Handbook

Ask students to apply the Before Reading stage of the reading process to the chapter from *Out of Africa* that their group has been assigned to read. Invite them to make preview notes on a Web or Magnet Summary.

For additional practice, have students set a purpose for and then preview the excerpt from Irvin Cobb's *When the Sea-Asp Stings,* which appears on pages 95–100 of *Student Applications Book 10*.

Assessment

Ask students:

■ What are a memoirist's two main purposes for writing?

■ How does the writer's purpose differ from the reader's purpose?

WEEK 10
Lesson 3   Reading a Memoir

For use with *Reader's Handbook* pages 216–221

Goals

In this lesson, students explore the During Reading strategies they can use to improve their comprehension of a memoir.

Teaching Focus

Background

There are two parts to the strategy of synthesizing. In the first part, the reader learns as much as he or she can about the general topics the writer is discussing. The second part involves combining details from the general topics and viewing the completed "portrait" the writer has created. In this lesson, you'll help students refine their understanding of synthesizing and then model how to use the strategy with a memoir.

Instruction

First, explain that most readers synthesize information without even realizing it. What the strategy of synthesizing does, however, is to focus their attention on the most important detail in a reading. In addition, it helps them understand how specific details fit together to create a cohesive whole. Next, ask a student to recall a reader's purpose for reading a memoir. Discuss During Reading strategies students can use to meet their purposes. Finish by asking students to do an active reading of the excerpt from *Out of Africa*. Have them make a Key Topic Notes organizer.

Teaching Approach

Use of the Handbook

Have students read silently the key topics listed in the left-hand column of the Key Topic Notes organizer on page 215. Point out that this is a general list of topics a memoirist might cover. Then read aloud the information on reading with a purpose and direct students to do a careful reading of the excerpt from *Out of Africa*. Students should make notes in their Key Topics organizers as they read. Finish with a brief discussion of why it's important for readers to connect to a memoir. Ask students to jot down some connection comments in their reading journals.

Extend the Handbook

Ask students to use the strategy of synthesizing to help them read their group's assigned chapter from *Out of Africa*. Invite them to make notes on a Web that is similar to the one on page 220. When they've finished, ask a member from each group to summarize the key events from the chapter.

Assessment

Ask students:

■ What is synthesizing and how can it help you get more from reading a memoir?

■ What are some reading tools that can help you synthesize?

After Reading a Memoir

For use with *Reader's Handbook* pages 223–224

Goals

Here students will discuss the organization of a memoir and how the After Reading stage of the reading process can help them process what they've read.

Teaching Focus

Background

Spend a few moments at the beginning of the lesson discussing the importance of making a personal connection to a memoir. Explain to students that connecting to the people, places, and events the writer describes can make the writer's reactions easier to understand. It can also help students more thoughtfully reflect upon the "portrait" the writer has created, thus making it easier for them to complete the After Reading steps of the reading process.

Instruction

Open the lesson with a discussion of the purpose and importance of connecting to a memoir. Then ask another student to review the After Reading steps of the reading process. Invite students to brainstorm a list of After Reading questions that might work well with a memoir. Have them compare their lists to the Looking Back list on page 223. Discuss the rereading strategy of visualizing and thinking aloud and how it can help students zero in on particular details they have missed on their first reading and patch up their comprehension of a memoir.

Teaching Approach

Use of the Handbook

Read aloud page 223. Discuss what readers do when they pause and reflect. Have students examine the Looking Back questions and apply them to Dinesen's memoir. Have a volunteer read aloud information on the rereading strategy students might use with this type of literature and the Remember strategies that come in handy with a memoir.

Extend the Handbook

Ask groups to choose one of the two activities discussed on page 224 and use it with the chapter they read from *Out of Africa*. When they've finished, have them present their work to the rest of the class. Encourage students to finish reading it outside of class.

Assessment

Ask students:

- What is the most important thing to do after reading a memoir?

- Why can the strategy of visualzing and thinking aloud be helpful after reading a memoir?

WEEK 11
Reading a News Story

For use with *Reader's Handbook* pages 181–192

Daily Lessons	Summary
Lesson 1 **Before Reading a** **News Story**	Review the Before Reading stage of the reading process and explore ways of using it with news stories.
Lesson 2 **Examining the Lead**	Help students understand the importance of a newspaper article's lead.
Lesson 3 **Reading Critically**	Explore the strategy of reading critically and discuss its uses with a news story.
Lesson 4 **Reflecting on a** **News Story**	Work with students as they reflect upon the facts and details of a news story. Discuss the rereading strategy of summarizing.

Lesson Resources

Overheads

For this lesson, use:

Overhead 18: Previewing a News Story

See *Student Applications Book* pages 74–83.

See *Teacher's Guide* pages 121–129.

See Website www.greatsource.com/rehand

Focus on Persuasive Writing

For use with *Reader's Handbook* pages 225–234

Daily Lessons	**Summary**
Lesson 1 **Persuasive Writing: Its Purpose**	Discuss with students the characteristics and purpose of persuasive writing. Have students recall examples of the genre.
Lesson 2 **Finding the Topic**	Introduce a three-step plan for understanding persuasive writing. Focus on Step 1, Find the topic.
Lesson 3 **Recognizing the Assertion**	Explore the importance of the author's assertion and how to make inferences about the author's viewpoint if it's not stated directly.
Lesson 4 **Evaluating the Argument**	Work with students as they learn to thoughtfully evaluate an author's support. Help them understand the kinds of After Reading strategies that work well with persuasive writing.

Lesson Resources

See *Student Applications Book 10* pages 105–106.

See *Teacher's Guide* pages 150–153.

See Website www.greatsource.com/rehand

Before Reading a News Story

For use with *Reader's Handbook* page 181–186

Goals

In this lesson, students apply the Before Reading stage of the reading process to a news story.

Teaching Focus

Background

News stories—as opposed to features and editorials—present facts and details about recent events. They often include quotes from witnesses and experts, as well as eyewitness testimony. The reader's job is to examine the facts given and then assess their validity. The reading process can help.

Instruction

Begin by explaining that the purpose of this lesson is to apply Before Reading strategies to a news story. Ask students, What is a news story? Where can you find this type of writing? What are its chief characteristics? Refine students' ideas as needed. Then ask volunteers to identify and explain each of the three steps of the Before Reading stage. Point out how each step works with a news story and how quickly the steps are covered. End by having students preview "Violent Images May Alter Kids' Brain Activity." Have them make notes on a Preview Chart similar to the one shown on page 75 of *Student Applications Book 10*.

Teaching Approach

Use of the Handbook

Direct students' attention to page 181. Have a volunteer read aloud the goals in the Goals box. Ask students, How would these goals be different for an editorial? How would they be different for an essay? Next, walk students through the information that appears under Set a Purpose and Preview. Discuss creating a plan for reading a news story and offer a brief explanation of the strategy of reading critically.

Extend the Handbook

Gather a variety of news stories from various sources: newspapers, magazines, and Internet news sites. Have each student choose one article and ask them to apply the three ideas learned in this part of the handbook. Discuss how using the ideas affected their understanding of the story.

Assessment

Ask students:

■ What is the purpose of a news story?

■ What does it mean to "read critically" and why is this a helpful strategy to use?

WEEK 11
Lesson 2
Examining the Lead

For use with *Reader's Handbook* pages 183, 188

Goals

In this lesson, students explore characteristics of a news story's lead.

Teaching Focus

Background

The lead is arguably the most important part of a news story. Here the writer identifies *who, what, where, when, why,* and *how.* Proficient readers know that a careful reading of the lead results in a more thorough understanding of the news story as a whole.

Instruction

Explain that the purpose of this lesson is to familiarize students with the lead of a news story. Ask for definitions of the term *lead* and then invite students to name its characteristics. Help them understand that good writers give 5 W's and H information up front so that newspaper readers can get the facts they need quickly. Invite students to examine the lead of "Violent Images May Alter Kids' Brain Activity." Ask students, Does the writer answer who, what, where, when, why, and how in her lead?

Teaching Approach

Use of the Handbook

If you feel students need extra help with the concept of a news story's lead, read aloud the first paragraph of the sample article on page 183. Walk students through the process of identifying components of the reporter's lead. Point out the organizational diagram on page 188 to help students understand the role of the lead in a news story.

For additional practice, direct students to complete pages 74–83 of *Student Applications Book 10.*

Extend the Handbook

Have students write their own lead for a news story. Ask them to begin by creating a 5 W's and H Organizer similar to the one on page 745 of the handbook. Have them use the organizer to help them write their leads.

Assessment

Ask students:

■ What is the purpose of the lead paragraph in a news story?

■ What are the 5 W's and H questions and how can they help you better understand the information in a news article?

WEEK 11
Lesson 3 ▸ Reading Critically

For use with *Reader's Handbook* pages 185–187

Goals

Here students explore the strategy of reading critically and discover how it can help them evaluate the reliability of the facts presented in a news story.

Teaching Focus

Background

Good readers question what they read, rather than blindly accept everything the author says. This is particularly important when reading news stories. The old adage that there are two sides to every story holds true for articles published in a newspaper as well. The strategy of reading critically helps readers evaluate information as they read to determine its fairness and accuracy.

Instruction

Begin by explaining that all news stories are biased to a degree—some more than others. Define the term *bias* for students and then explain that bias occurs in news stories when the writer presents opinions as facts or leaves out information that supports the other side of an issue. Introduce the strategy of reading critically and help students understand that it involves looking at what is and what is not presented and what bias, if any, comes in the selection of the facts.

Teaching Approach

Use of the Handbook

Ask students to turn to page 726 of the Strategy Handbook and read the explanation of reading critically. Then have them read page 185 for specific information on how to use the strategy with a news story. Point out the Critical Reading Chart on page 186. Explain that you'd like them to copy the chart in their reading journals and use it for their notes as they read "Violent Images May Alter Kids' Brain Activity." At the end of the lesson, have students do their careful reading of the article. After they finish reading and taking notes, students should compare what they wrote with the completed chart on page 187.

Extend the Handbook

Have students finish reading the newspaper article they started in the previous lesson. Ask them to apply the strategy of reading critically to the article, using a Critical Reading Chart for their notes. Check students' work to be sure they have a clear understanding of the strategy and how it is used.

Assessment

Ask students:

■ What is bias?

■ What does it mean to do a critical reading of a news story?

■ What are the five critical reading questions to ask when reading a news story?

WEEK 11
Lesson 4 — Reflecting on a News Story

For use with *Reader's Handbook* pages 188–192

Goals

Here students learn the organization of news stories and how and why they should take the time to reflect on what they've read.

Teaching Focus

Background

Many news stories follow a standard organization called an *inverted pyramid*. (Feature writers usually follow a straightforward pyramid structure with the most important details appearing at the end of the article.) Understanding the structure of a news story can help students more effectively reflect on what they've read. In this lesson, you'll discuss organization and then make a link to the Pause and Reflect step of the reading process. In addition, you'll discuss techniques students can use to remember what they've read.

Instruction

Discuss with students how a news story is organized. Explain the term *inverted pyramid*. Draw a large pyramid on the board and ask students to plug parts of "Violent Images" into the pyramid. Then ask the class to write brief summaries of the After Reading stage of the reading process. When they've finished, review the characteristics of summarizing and explain that it can be a rereading strategy. Have students create Summary Notes for the handbook's news story. Then ask them to compare what they wrote to the completed Summary Notes on page 191.

Teaching Approach

Use of the Handbook

Have students read page 188 and use what they've learned to help you finish the pyramid. Then direct their attention to page 189. Discuss the purpose of connecting to a news story and explore the connections students made to "Violent Images." Concentrate on elements of the After Reading stage of the reading process. Have students read page 190. After they compare their Summary Notes to those in the handbook, read aloud the two activities listed under Remember.

Extend the Handbook

Ask students to finish the article they began writing in a previous lesson. Have them exchange drafts with a partner and comment on the ways in which the writing might be strengthened.

Assessment

Ask students:

■ What are the key features of an inverted pyramid structure?

■ Why is it important to reflect on what you've read in a news story?

Persuasive Writing: Its Purpose

WEEK 12
Lesson 1

For use with *Reader's Handbook* page 225, 250

Goals

Here students explore the characteristics and purpose of persuasive writing.

Teaching Focus

Background

By definition, persuasive writing is writing that attempts to prove something is true or convince you to adopt the same viewpoint as the writer. Unlike other forms of nonfiction, persuasive writing is biased writing. The writer presents a single viewpoint or opinion and works hard to convince the reader of its validity.

Instruction

Begin by asking students to tell what they know about persuasive writing. Ask about its purpose and where you might find it. Then find out what students know about its organization. Help students understand that good persuasive writing contains a topic, a clear opinion statement, and at least three supporting details.

Teaching Approach

Use of the Handbook

After your general discussion of persuasive writing, have students turn to page 250 of the *Reader's Handbook* and read the entry for Assertion or Viewpoint. Discuss how the excerpt from Rachel Carson's essay is an example of persuasive writing. Then have students turn to page 225 and begin working on the unit. Have a volunteer read aloud the introductory paragraphs. Ask students to study the list of actions persuasive writing can ask you to do. They may want to refer to this list as they make their way through the unit.

Extend the Handbook

Reinforce the teaching in the handbook by having students complete pages 105–106 of *Student Applications Book 10*. As a first step, have them preview the Eastern Ballet article (page 105). Then ask them to follow the steps outlined. You'll notice that these steps are modeled on the handbook's Three-step Plan for understanding persuasive writing.

Assessment

Ask students:

■ What is the purpose of persuasive writing?

■ Why do you think the strategy of reading critically works well with persuasive writing?

WEEK 12
Lesson 2

Finding the Topic

For use with *Reader's Handbook* pages 225–228

Goals

Here you'll introduce and then discuss a three-step plan for understanding persuasive writing.

Teaching Focus

Background

A well-composed argument is made up of three parts: the topic, the assertion or opinion statement, and supporting details. In addition, good persuasive writers acknowledge and then refute the opposition at some point in the body of the argument. Refuting the opposing argument can be as simple as, "Although supporters say that sugar is good for your health, . . ."

Instruction

Your primary purpose in this lesson is to teach students techniques for finding the topic of a persuasive piece. Begin by discussing the three parts of an argument. Then write these three steps on the board: Step 1: Find the topic; Step 2: Find the assertion; Step 3: Decide what you think about the argument. Tell students that in this lesson, you'll be focusing on Step 1 of the plan for understanding an argument.

Teaching Approach

Use of the Handbook

Have students read the goals listed on page 225 and brainstorm additional goals they could add. Then have students turn to page 226 and examine the Three-step Plan for understanding an argument. Post the plan on the board and encourage students to refer to it over the course of the week. During the second half of the lesson, ask students to concentrate on finding the topic in a piece of persuasive writing. Explain that readers often can find information about the topic of the argument at the Preview stage of the reading process. Later, have students preview "Appearances Are Destructive" on pages 227–228. Ask students to make notes about the topic of the argument in their reading journals.

Extend the Handbook

Gather samples of persuasive writing, such as newspaper editorials or letters to the editor. (You also may want to include examples of student writing.) Divide students into small groups and ask them to preview the piece. Have them create and then use a Preview Chart similar to the one on page 229 of the *Reader's Handbook.*

Assessment

Ask students:

■ What are the three parts of an effective argument?

■ What question should you ask yourself if you're having trouble figuring out a persuasive writer's topic?

WEEK 12
Lesson 3

Recognizing the Assertion

For use with *Reader's Handbook* pages 226–229

Goals

In this lesson, students learn how to find the writer's assertion in a piece of persuasive writing.

Teaching Focus

Background

Good writers know that a piece of persuasive writing is only as strong as the opinion it advances. This means that the writer's statement of opinion (called the *assertion* or *viewpoint*) must be clear, to the point, and easy to understand. In this lesson, you'll teach students how to spot the assertion in a piece of persuasive writing.

Instruction

Ask a student to review aloud the Three-step Plan for understanding an argument. Tell the class that here you will be focusing on Step 2, Find the assertion. Have a volunteer define the term *assertion*. Then have students copy this formula in their reading journals:

> Topic + What the author says about the topic = The assertion

Teaching Approach

Use of the Handbook

Rather than teach a long lesson on assertions and how they are formed, simply ask students to do a careful reading of Mathabane's essay on 227–228. Ask them to watch for a clear opinion statement or clues that indicate how Mathabane feels about the topic. When students have finished reading, gather them for a whole-class discussion of Mathabane's assertion. Ask students, How does Mathabane feel about dress codes? What does he like or dislike about them? If there is disagreement, ask students to return to the essay and substantiate their answers.

Extend the Handbook

Ask students to do an active reading of the piece of persuasive writing they previewed in the previous lesson. Ask them to highlight information about the topic, underline the author's assertion (or clues about the assertion), and keep an eye out for supporting details. Have them model their notes on the ones shown in the handbook on pages 227–228.

Assessment

Ask students:

■ What is the difference between the topic and assertion in persuasive writing?

■ Why is it important that a persuasive writer support the assertion?

102

WEEK 12
Lesson 4   Evaluating the Argument

For use with *Reader's Handbook* pages 229–234

Goals

Here students learn how and why they should evaluate a writer's argument.

Teaching Focus

Background

Readers often make the mistake of evaluating the argument first, before they fully understand it. This is why it's important that you help students see that it's impossible to evaluate a piece of persuasive writing if you don't thoroughly understand the writer's argument. In addition, students should know that, for their criticism to be valid, they must substantiate it with good, solid reasons.

Instruction

Before you get into Step 3, discuss the role of the opposing viewpoint in persuasive writing. Have students skim Mathabane's essay on page 228 and find where he addresses the opposition. Point out that this technique of explaining and then refuting the opposing argument makes the writer's assertion all the stronger. Ask students, What details does Mathabane offer to prove that his assertion is correct? Does he offer several different types of details, or are they all from one source? Would you say his support is adequate? These are the kinds of questions students should ask when evaluating an argument.

Teaching Approach

Use of the Handbook

Have students refer to pages 227–228 when discussing Mathabane's support for his assertion. Explain to students that good writers use details from a variety of sources. Then direct students' attention to the discussion of reading critically on page 229. Discuss why this strategy is particularly good to use with persuasive writing. Point out the Argument Chart and explain how to use it. Then divide the class into small groups and have them read and discuss the After Reading strategies they might use with persuasive writing.

Extend the Handbook

Ask students to evaluate the persuasive writing they read in the previous lesson. Have them create an Argument Chart and use it assess the writer's argument. Reconvene and ask each group, What is your opinion of the writer's assertion? Would you say the author's support is strong and convincing? Has the author's argument changed your view of the topic?

Assessment

Ask students:

■ Why is it important to evaluate a persuasive writer's argument? How do you do this?

■ What After Reading strategies might you use with persuasive writing?

Elements of Nonfiction

For use with *Reader's Handbook* pages 246–263

Daily Lessons	Summary
Lesson 1 **Author's Purpose and Assertion**	Reinforce and refine students' understanding of the terms *author's purpose* and *assertion* and their relevance to nonfiction.
Lesson 2 **Deductive and Inductive Reasoning**	Help students explore deductive vs. inductive reasoning and the impact each can have on the structure and organization of a nonfiction piece.
Lesson 3 **Irony and Satire**	Activate prior knowledge of irony and satire and how they affect the tone of the work.
Lesson 4 **Main Idea and Supporting Details**	Refine students' understanding of how to find the main idea and supporting details in a nonfiction piece.

Lesson Resources

See *Teacher's Guide* pages 159–176.

See Website www.greatsource.com/rehand

See *Test Book* for multiple-choice and short-answer tests.

For more practice, see also *Sourcebook* Grade 10, pages 124–133, 134–142.

WEEK 14
Elements of Fiction

For use with *Reader's Handbook* pages 366–385

Daily Lessons	Summary
Lesson 1 **Flashback and Foreshadowing**	Have students skim this section of the *Reader's Handbook* and consider its purpose. In addition, they'll discuss why writers of fiction use flashback and foreshadowing in their stories.
Lesson 2 **Irony**	Refine students' understanding of irony and how it can affect the tone of a story, novel, or play.
Lesson 3 **Plot and Subplot**	Discuss the interrelationship between plot and subplot in a work of fiction.
Lesson 4 **Tone and Mood**	Help students explore the ways in which writers establish mood and tone in fiction.

Lesson Resources

See *Teacher's Guide* pages 233–249

See Website www.greatsource.com/rehand

See *Test Book* for multiple-choice and short-answer tests.

WEEK 13
Lesson 1

Author's Purpose and Assertion

For use with *Reader's Handbook* pages 250–251

Goals

Here students will review what they know about author's purpose and the four major reasons an author might have for writing.

Teaching Focus

Background

The Elements of Nonfiction section of the handbook has seventeen terms. In this lesson, you'll discuss two of the most essential: assertion and author's purpose. In the lessons that follow, you'll teach several other terms, including *deductive and inductive reasoning, irony, main idea,* and *supporting details.*

Instruction

Begin with a discussion of author's purpose. Ask students, What are the four basic reasons an author might write a book, article, or essay? Help them articulate author's purpose as one of the following: to explain or inform, to entertain, to persuade, and to reveal an interesting truth. Offer examples from the *Reader's Handbook* and literature anthologies as needed. Then turn to a discussion of assertion. Ask a student to define the term and explain its importance in persuasive writing. Use page 250 in the Elements of Nonfiction to support your teaching.

Teaching Approach

Use of the Handbook

Ask students to examine page 246. Have them note unfamiliar terms so that you might explore them in some detail later. Then have a volunteer read aloud the page 251. Next, direct students to read silently the information on assertion on page 250. Discuss the types of writing in which a reader might encounter an assertion. If there's time, review other nonfiction terms such as *bias, connotation* and *denotation,* and *rhetorical questions.*

Extend the Handbook

Ask students to bring to class examples of persuasive writing. Have small groups discuss author's purpose and find the assertion in each example.

Assessment

Ask students:

■ What are the four main reasons a nonfiction writer has for writing?

■ How would you define the term *assertion?*

106

WEEK 13
Lesson 2

Deductive and Inductive Reasoning

For use with *Reader's Handbook* pages 254–255

Goals

In this lesson, students will explore deductive and inductive reasoning and discuss the effect they have on the structure and organization of a work.

Teaching Focus

Background

Critical readers know the value of thinking like a scientist when reading nonfiction. They read the title, preview the piece, and then form a kind of prediction about what they expect to learn. They also track the organization of the writing to make it easier to locate the writer's most important ideas. Understanding the differences between inductive and deductive reasoning can help a reader follow the writer's line of thought from beginning to end.

Instruction

Begin by explaining that deductive reasoning refers to a way of thinking that moves from the general (the premise) to the specific (the conclusion). Inductive reasoning begins with specific details and ends with a general conclusion. To help students differentiate between the two, focus on the examples on pages 254–255.

Teaching Approach

Use of the Handbook

Have a volunteer read aloud page 254. Make notes on the board. Next, have another student read aloud page 255. Once again, make some general notes on the board. Ask students to explore both deductive and inductive thinking in a Magnet Summary in their reading journals. (Refer students to page 747 if they need help with Magnet Summaries.) Finish with a discussion of how deductive vs. inductive reasoning can affect the overall structure and organization of a work.

Extend the Handbook

Ask small groups to skim their textbooks, class newspapers, and other nonfiction texts for examples of inductive and deductive reasoning. Ask group members to discuss the literature and explain the clues they found that helped them identify the type of reasoning the writer uses.

Assessment

Ask students:

■ What is the difference between deductive and inductive reasoning?

■ How can understanding these terms help you become a more effective reader of nonfiction?

WEEK 13
Lesson 3 — Irony and Satire

For use with *Reader's Handbook* pages 256, 261

Goals

In this lesson, students refine their understanding of irony and satire and discuss their uses in nonfiction writing.

Teaching Focus

Background

Irony is a humorous or sarcastic way of saying the opposite of what is really meant. Among other reasons, nonfiction writers use irony to lighten the mood, create the tone, and establish the main idea of a piece of writing. Satire differs from irony in that its primary purpose is to ridicule a human weakness or vice. As a secondary purpose, writers use satire to correct or change the subject of the satiric attack. Writers who use irony tend to do so in small doses, while writers using satire tend to stay in satiric form from the beginning to the end of the piece.

Instruction

Ask students to define the terms *irony* and *satire*. Refine their definitions as needed using the handbook to support your discussion. Next, ask students to name various examples of irony and satire with which they're familiar. Have volunteers explain the effect of the irony or satire on the piece of writing as a whole and the main idea in particular.

Teaching Approach

Use of the Handbook

Ask a volunteer to read aloud the example of irony shown on page 256. Discuss the example as a class. Then direct students' attention to the discussion of satire (page 261) and read aloud the clip from the Dave Barry column. Ask students, How is this an example of satire? What is Barry's subject, or "target"?

Extend the Handbook

Ask students to write a paragraph in which they explain the uses of irony or satire in nonfiction. Have them open with a definition of the term they want to discuss and then provide an example from their own reading.

Assessment

Ask students:

■ What is irony?

■ What is satire?

■ What effect do irony and satire generally have on a piece of writing?

**WEEK 13
Lesson 4**

Main Idea and Supporting Details

For use with *Reader's Handbook* pages 259, 262

Goals

In this lesson, students will discuss the importance of finding and understanding the main idea and supporting details in a work of nonfiction.

Teaching Focus

Background

Readers often confuse the topic of a piece of writing with its main idea. In this lesson, you'll want to begin by establishing a clear definition of the term *main idea* and then discuss the ways a reader finds the main idea and supporting details in a text. Much of what you discuss here will help students with the slightly more complex topic of theme.

Instruction

Begin by making the following distinction between topic and main idea: The topic of a nonfiction piece is who or what the author is discussing. The main idea of the piece is the author's feelings about the topic. Encourage students to use this formula:

Topic + what the author says or thinks about it = the main idea

After presenting the definition for and examples of main idea, begin your lesson on supporting details. Point out that good nonfiction writers know to support their main idea with three or more compelling details. Students should understand that if the support is not adequate, or the details are not credible, then the piece of writing is considered flawed.

Teaching Approach

Use of the Handbook

Review the definition for main idea and then direct students' attention to page 259. Ask them to read the paragraph from "To Be Young, Gifted and Black" and think about the main idea of the paragraph, as well as the details Hansberry uses to support her main idea.

Extend the Handbook

Ask students to create a Main Idea Organizer for the excerpt from "The Lantern-Bearers," on page 262.

Assessment

Ask students:

■ What is the difference between the topic and main idea?

■ Why is it important for a writer to support a main idea with three or more details?

Flashback and Foreshadowing

For use with *Reader's Handbook* pages 366–385

Goals

In this lesson, students will preview the Elements of Fiction section and then discuss the purpose of foreshadowing and flashback in a work of fiction.

Teaching Focus

Background

The purpose of the Elements of Fiction section is to strengthen students' understanding of key literary terms they will use when writing about or discussing fiction. You may want to teach a mini-lesson on each entry, or you may want to teach the elements discussed here and have students read about the others on their own. In either case, allow students to preview the entire section. Ask them to note terms they would like to read about in more detail.

Instruction

Focus on the elements of *flashback* and *foreshadowing*. First, go over the examples and define the terms. Tell students that flashback is an interruption in the sequence of the narrative. Its purpose is to show something that happened before a particular point in the narrative. Then explain that foreshadowing provides hints early in a story that anticipate what's to come. Its purpose is to increase suspense, contribute to mood, and make the ending credible.

Teaching Approach

Use of the Handbook

Use the handbook to support your discussion of these two literary terms. Have students turn to page 373 and read silently the excerpt from *All Quiet on the Western Front*. Discuss Remarque's flashback. Ask students, What is its purpose? What does it tell you about the narrator? Then as a class read the Description and Definition. Next, have students read the excerpt from "A Good Man Is Hard to Find" (page 374). Discuss O'Connor's use of foreshadowing. What is its purpose?

Extend the Handbook

Brainstorm a list of books and movies with memorable flashbacks. Ask students to choose one work and write how flashback is used. Repeat the activity with foreshadowing.

Assessment

Ask students:

■ What is flashback? Why do authors use it?

■ What is foreshadowing? What purpose does it serve?

WEEK 14
Lesson 2 Irony

For use with *Reader's Handbook* page 376

Goals

In this lesson, students learn the role irony plays in the plot of a story.

Teaching Focus

Background

Irony is a difficult concept for some students to grasp—perhaps because they haven't been exposed to enough of it. The confusion might also derive from three different types of irony: *verbal irony, irony of situation,* and *dramatic irony*. An example of verbal irony is when a person says one thing but does another. (Shakespeare used a great deal of verbal irony.) Situational irony occurs when events turn out contrary to what is expected. Dramatic irony describes a situation in which the audience of the play knows more about a character's situation than he or she does. In this lesson, you'll discuss all three types and their effect on a work as a whole.

Instruction

Open the lesson by explaining that the general definition for *irony* is "the contrast between what seems to be and what really is." Then list the three types of irony on the board and discuss them one at a time. Provide examples from students' English textbook or literature anthology if possible. After your discussion, reinforce what students have learned by having them read the mini-lesson on irony on page 376.

Teaching Approach

Use of the Handbook

Have students turn to page 376 and ask the class to read silently the excerpt from "Indian Education." When they have finished, discuss the description of irony and how it applies to the excerpt. End by discussing the impact irony can have on the tone and mood of a work.

Extend the Handbook

Ask students to reflect on the literary element of irony in their reading journals. Have them quickwrite for a minute or two an example of irony and then read what they've written.

Assessment

Ask students:

■ What are the three types of irony?

■ What effect does irony generally have on a story or play?

WEEK 14
Lesson 3 — Plot and Subplot

For use with *Reader's Handbook* page 378

Goals

In this lesson, students build understanding of the relationship between a main plot and its subplots.

Teaching Focus

Background

Plot is the sequence of interrelated incidents that present and then resolve a conflict. A well-constructed plot has five parts: exposition, rising action, climax, falling action, and resolution (or denouement). Some stories, especially the more complex ones, will have one or more subplots that unfold alongside the plot. In most cases, the subplot will share one or more characters with the main plot. Very often the central conflict in a subplot will occur at approximately the same time as the central conflict of the main plot. By the end of the story, the subplot or subplots are usually resolved within the main plot.

Instruction

Have a volunteer give a plot summary of a well-known novel, such as *Tom Sawyer*. Ask other volunteers to summarize what happens in the subplots. Discuss the relationship between plot and subplots in this novel and in general. Be sure students understand that just because the subplot is subordinate to the main plot it doesn't necessarily mean the subplot will be less interesting.

Teaching Approach

Use of the Handbook

Ask students turn to page 378 and read silently the plot summary that follows. Explain that, in *Bless Me, Ultima,* Antonio's adventures with the Gold Carp, crazy neighbor, and first year of school are all subplots to the main plot that centers around Antonio and Ultima. Finish the lesson by asking a volunteer to read aloud the description and definition on page 378.

Extend the Handbook

Recall with students a work they've read that is heavy with subplots. (A novel by Charles Dickens would work well for the activity.) Draw a Plot Diagram on the board and ask students to help you record events from the plot and one of the subplots. Add additional subplot columns if you have time.

Assessment

Ask students:

■ What is the difference between a plot and a subplot?

■ What can subplots add to a work of fiction?

WEEK 14
Lesson 4

Tone and Mood

For use with *Reader's Handbook* page 385

Goals

Here students will explore the characteristics of tone and mood and the effect they can have on a story as a whole.

Teaching Focus

Background

Tone and mood can have a profound effect on a work and the enjoyment a reader derives from it. Making inferences about tone and mood can deepen students' ability to understand and evaluate the work and its themes.

Instruction

Explore what students know about tone and mood. Work with them to establish definitions and to differentiate the two. Explain that *tone* is used to describe an author's attitude toward the subject, characters, or reader, while *mood* refers to the general atmosphere of the work. The term *mood* can also be used to describe the effect the work as a whole has on a reader. Finish the lesson by brainstorming examples of books with a strong tone or mood.

Teaching Approach

Use of the Handbook

Have students turn to page 385. Ask a volunteer to read aloud the excerpt from Liam O'Flaherty's novel. Ask students, What is the tone of O'Flaherty's writing? What is the mood? Help students see the word choices and sentence structures that create the matter-of-fact tone of the writing. Then discuss the mood of suspense. Ask students, How does O'Flaherty create this mood? Explain that later, students will be expected to identify the tone and mood of a short story entitled "Powder" (pages 270–275) and in an excerpt from the novel *All Quiet on the Western Front* (pages 291–301).

Extend the Handbook

Divide the class into small groups. Ask students to gather examples of works that have memorable tones or moods. Have students agree on one work to analyze in some detail. Ask them, What is the story mostly about? What is the tone like? What is the mood like? What does the tone or mood remind you of? Invite representatives to report on their discussion to the rest of the class.

Assessment

Ask students:

■ What is the difference between *tone* and *mood?*

■ How can making inferences about tone and mood help you better understand the work?

WEEK 15

Reading a Short Story

For use with *Reader's Handbook* pages 267–287

Daily Lessons	Summary
Lesson 1 **Before Reading a** **Short Story**	Activate students' prior knowledge of the genre. Discuss how the reading process can help students get more from a short story.
Lesson 2 **Reading a Short Story**	Review active reading methods and explore the importance of becoming involved with the plot of a short story.
Lesson 3 **Using Reading Tools** **with Short Stories**	Discuss various reading tools that work well with fiction in general and short stories in particular.
Lesson 4 **After Reading a** **Short Story**	Work with students as they use the rereading strategy of close reading with a short story. Finish with a discussion of how to retain key aspects of a story.

Lesson Resources

Overheads

For this lesson, use:
Overheads 24 and 25: Previewing a Short Story.

See *Student Applications Book 10* pages 110–123.

See *Teacher's Guide* pages 178–188.

See *Test Book* for multiple-choice and short-answer tests.

See Website www.greatsource.com/rehand

For more practice, see also *Sourcebook* Grade 10, pages 112–124; *Daybook* Grade 10, pages 21–34.

WEEK 16
Focus on Setting

For use with *Reader's Handbook* pages 323–331

Daily Lessons	**Summary**
Lesson 1 **The Importance of Setting**	Present an overview of the characteristics of setting and the effect it can have on the characters, plot, and mood of a story.
Lesson 2 **Setting and Mood**	Explore in some detail the relationship between setting and mood. Ask students to provide examples from their own reading.
Lesson 3 **Setting and Characters**	Discuss with students how writers can use setting as a vehicle for character revelation.
Lesson 4 **Setting and Plot**	Work with students to activate prior knowledge of plot and help them understand the effect a story's setting can have on its plot.

Lesson Resources

See *Student Applications Book 10* pages 139–140.
See *Teacher's Guide* pages 206–210.
See *Test Book* for multiple-choice and short-answer tests.
See Website www.greatsource.com/rehand

For more practice, see also *Sourcebook* Grade 10, pages 57–63; *Daybook* Grade 10, pages 139–140.

WEEK 15
Lesson 1

Before Reading a Short Story

For use with *Reader's Handbook* pages 267–277, 280

Goals

In this lesson, students set a purpose, plan, and preview before reading a short story.

Teaching Focus

Background

Reading fiction can provide students with a better understanding of the world and an appreciation of literature as art. Short stories are less intimidating than other forms of fiction. They typically deal with a single episode involving a limited number of characters. Their brevity presents readers with the challenge of culling the theme from a short plot and small cast of characters.

Instruction

Have volunteers discuss short stories that they have read. Ask them to describe how the short story is similar to other genres. Ask students, How is it different? Refer to How Stories Are Organized on page 280 of the *Reader's Handbook* and explain the common structure of short stories. Then ask students to think about how they would go about setting a purpose, previewing, and planning to read a short story.

Teaching Approach

Use of the Handbook

Explain to students that they will be reading "Powder" by Tobias Wolff during the next four lessons. Offer background about the story and the author. Ask them to read independently pages 267–269 and 276–277, which describe how to preview and set a purpose for reading a short story. Next, have them preview the story (pages 270–275). Ask volunteers why the strategy of synthesizing might be helpful with short stories.

Extend the Handbook

Have students make a series of predictions about the setting, plot, and characters of "Powder." Invite volunteers to share their predictions with the class.

Assessment

Ask students:

■ What steps are needed before reading a short story?

■ How do you preview a short story?

WEEK 15
Lesson 2
Reading a Short Story

For use with *Reader's Handbook* pages 277–278, 281–282.

Goals

In this lesson, students learn strategies for reading and connecting to short stories.

Teaching Focus

Background

Although students may not need much coaxing to read short stories, it can help if they know strategies for getting the most out of them. This lesson introduces students to the reading strategies of synthesizing and the idea connecting to stories they read.

Instruction

Ask students to brainstorm how they would apply various active reading tools that they've learned in other units—such as using the 5 W's and H and visualizing and thinking—to reading short stories. After you discuss their ideas, read the description of synthesizing on page 277. Stress that paying attention to elements of a short story allows them to arrive at an informed interpretation of it. Then, read aloud the information under the head Connect on page 281. Point out that whether they empathize with a character or relate to the action of a story, making a personal connection can enhance their understanding and enjoyment of short stories.

Teaching Approach

Use of the Handbook

Ask students to review the information about purpose on pages 276–278. Then have them read "Powder." Ask them to draw their own Fiction Organizers and take notes while reading. Encourage them to use other active reading strategies that they find useful. After students finish reading, ask volunteers to discuss what they included in their Fiction Organizer. Make a chart on the board to record their observations.

Extend the Handbook

Ask students either to create a Making Connections Chart in their journals or write a free-form journal entry about "Powder." Have volunteers read their journal entries. Consider writing your own journal entry to share with students.

Assessment

Ask students:

▪ What is the purpose of synthesizing?

▪ What other reading tools might be helpful when reading short stories?

▪ Why is it important to make a personal connection to a short story?

Using Reading Tools with Short Stories

WEEK 15
Lesson 3

For use with *Reader's Handbook* pages 278–282

Goals

In this lesson, students learn about reading tools they can use to keep track of various short-story elements.

Teaching Focus

Background

Although short stories are relatively brief in form, they are often complex in scope and meaning. In addition to keeping track of the action, readers of short stories have to focus on a number of literary elements, including characters, setting, plot, tone, and style. The various graphic organizers presented in this lesson enable students to meet their purpose for reading and to make a personal connection to short stories.

Instruction

Direct students to pages 278–282 of the *Reader's Handbook*. Familiarize students with the five types of graphic organizers that work well with short stories—Fiction Organizers, Cause-Effect Organizers, Character Development Charts, Plot Diagrams, and Making Connections Charts. Discuss the ways in which each type of graphic organizer can help students achieve their purpose for reading and synthesize various elements of the story. Explain that these graphic organizers also work with other forms of literature.

Teaching Approach

Use of the Handbook

Divide the class into three groups. Give them a chance to skim "Powder" once more. Then assign each group a different type of graphic organizer to complete. Later, reconvene as a class and have students explain how using the graphic organizer shaped their understanding of the story.

Extend the Handbook

In their reading journals, students can reflect upon two reading tools they think are particularly useful with short stories. Ask them to identify the organizer, describe how it is used, and explain why it is effective.

Assessment

Ask students:

■ What reading tools are helpful in understanding short stories?

■ Why is it important to make a personal connection to a short story?

118

After Reading a Short Story

WEEK 15 Lesson 4

For use with *Reader's Handbook* pages 283–287

Goals

Here students learn how the After Reading stage of the reading process applies to short stories.

Teaching Focus

Background

Short stories can resonate so strongly that readers sometimes remember them for years to come. (For example, at any given time, you could probably recall in some detail the main literary elements of "The Lottery" by Shirley Jackson, "The Pit and the Pendulum" by Edgar Allan Poe, and "The Gift of the Magi" by O. Henry.) In this lesson, students learn that pausing, reflecting, and rereading can deepen their understanding of short stories.

Instruction

Review the steps of the After Reading stage of the reading process. Explain that pausing and reflecting on a short story after reading can help students clarify in their minds key themes in the story. Next, explain that rereading allows students to pay more attention to how and why the story followed a certain course and to revise their purpose for reading. Discuss how a Close Reading Organizer, Setting Chart, and Venn Diagram can reinforce their understanding of a story. Finally, discuss strategies students can use to remember what they've read.

Teaching Approach

Use of the Handbook

Have students respond in their journals to the Looking Back questions on page 283 of the handbook. Ask them to reread parts or all of the story and use a Close Reading Organizer to record their thoughts. Then ask students to look at the Setting Chart on page 285 and the Venn Diagram on page 286. Discuss the importance of rereading short stories and what students can hope to gain from it.

Extend the Handbook

Divide the class into two or three groups and ask them to discuss their reflections on "Powder." Suggest that they use either the questions under the heading Talk about It on page 286 or choose their own topics for discussion. Then ask students to perform the sequel-writing exercise described on page 287 of the handbook.

Assessment

Ask students:

■ What strategies can you use after reading a short story?

■ Why is it sometimes necessary to reread parts of short story?

WEEK 16
Lesson 1

The Importance of Setting

For use with *Reader's Handbook* pages 323–325

Goals

In this lesson, students gain a deeper understanding of the role that setting plays in a work of fiction.

Teaching Focus

Background

As you know, the time, place, and circumstances in which the action of a story occurs comprise the setting. In some works, the setting plays a starring role that rivals even the main character. In others, the setting is somewhat incidental. Whether a major or minor part of the story, the setting complements the characters and plot and contributes to the mood of a story.

Instruction

Students should readily define the word *setting*. Encourage them to consider various times and places that might constitute a story's settings, including actual places; imaginary planets; and various times of the day in the past, present, and future. Then introduce students to two new terms: *general setting* and *immediate setting*. Explain that general settings are the overall locations and periods in which the action of the story takes place. Immediate settings are the more specific milieus of various scenes in a story. The setting changes in Tobias Wolff's short story "Powder" will show students that both general and immediate settings can change at least once in a novel or story.

Teaching Approach

Use of the Handbook

Discuss clues authors can use to reveal the setting. Explain that students should note changes in the setting throughout the work. A change in the setting can signal a change in the action. Ask students to read page 324 of the *Reader's Handbook,* which has a passage from Alan Paton's novel *Cry, the Beloved Country.* Ask volunteers to distinguish between the general setting (Johannesburg, South Africa) and the immediate setting. Then focus students' attention on the close reading strategy explored on page 325. Explain how the Inference Chart can help readers track and interpret descriptive details about time and place.

Extend the Handbook

Ask students to write a journal entry about the immediate and general settings in "Powder." Invite volunteers to read their entries to the class.

Assessment

Ask students:

■ Why is the setting of a story or novel important?

■ In what ways can the strategy of close reading help you explore the setting of a work?

WEEK 16
Lesson 2
Setting and Mood

For use with *Reader's Handbook* pages 326–327

Goals

In this lesson, students discover how setting contributes to the mood of a story.

Teaching Focus

Background

Setting and mood are intimately connected. Without palpable details about the time and place of a story, readers cannot get a full sense its mood. The setting helps put readers in touch with the atmosphere that pervades a work and often foreshadows twists in the plot. This lesson exposes students to the connection between setting and mood and shows them a graphic organizer they can use to explore the interconnection between these two elements.

Instruction

Have volunteers brainstorm the term *mood*. Write their thoughts on the board. Then define the word for them. Ask volunteers to think about how the setting of a story can evoke specific feelings in readers. Offer examples from stories students have read in the past. Then ask the class to think about the general and immediate settings of "Powder" and the mood of the story. What connections do they see between setting and mood?

Teaching Approach

Use of the Handbook

Ask students to review the information about setting and mood on page 326 of the handbook. Then have them read silently the excerpt from *Cry, the Beloved Country*. When they finish, discuss the mood of this passage. Next, direct their attention to the Magnet Summary on page 327. Point out that this graphic organizer can help them explore the interplay between setting and mood in a story. Finally, have students read the section on page 327 about how authors use sensory details to delineate mood and setting.

Extend the Handbook

Divide students into three groups. Have them create a Magnet Summary that examines the mood in "Powder." Encourage them to work with any part of the story that they wish. Then reconvene the group and have students discuss their charts. Compare what each group chose as its focus.

Assessment

Ask students:

■ Why is it important for authors to set the mood of a story?

■ In what ways does the setting create a mood?

■ How can a Magnet Summary help you identify the mood of a story?

WEEK 16
Lesson 3
Setting and Character

For use with *Reader's Handbook* page 328

Goals

In this lesson, students explore how authors use setting to reveal details about a character's personality.

Teaching Focus

Background

The way that characters react to their surroundings can give clues about their aspirations, fears, strengths, and weaknesses. In addition, the way that the setting influences various characters in a story can shed light on differences in their personalities. This lesson shows how paying attention to characters' interaction with their environment can enhance a reader's understanding of the characters and of the story.

Instruction

Have students discuss the connection between setting and character. Write their ideas on the board. Then explain the various ways that the setting can reveal the personalities of characters. Use examples about one of your favorite fictional characters. Ask students to read page 328 and examine the Inference Chart one student made for *Cry, the Beloved Country*. Discuss what they learned about Gertrude and Kumalo.

Teaching Approach

Use of the Handbook

Once again, ask students to recall the various settings in "Powder" (pages 270–275). Ask them to think about what the father's and son's reactions to the setting tells us about them. What does the setting reveal about personality differences between the father and son? Have students work in pairs to create an Inference Chart for one of the settings in "Powder." Then come together as a class to discuss their inferences. Ask students, How did considering the influence of setting on the father and son deepen your understanding of "Powder"?

Extend the Handbook

For additional practice, have students consider their favorite fictional character again. After considering the character's reaction to the setting, what inferences can they make about the character's personality?

Assessment

Ask students:

■ How do setting and characters influence one another?

■ How can an Inference Chart help you understand the relationship between setting and character?

WEEK 16
Lesson 4   Setting and Plot

For use with *Reader's Handbook* pages 329–331

Goals

Here students will review what they've learned about plot, explore the relationship between setting and plot, and learn to evaluate the role of setting in a story.

Teaching Focus

Background

The setting of a story can serve yet another indispensable purpose for readers—namely, it can point to new developments in a story's plot. A change in setting often signals a shift in the direction of the story. Perhaps a character is about to face a challenge or a moment of truth. A new setting also might portend a resolution in the central or ancillary conflicts. In this lesson, students learn how to study the setting and explore the link between it and plot.

Instruction

Now that students understand the relationship between setting, mood, and character, discuss how setting and plot are intertwined. Then explain how setting or changes in setting can affect the plot of a work. Provide an example of an instance in which the setting shapes the action of the story. (You may recall that the plot of many historical novels is driven by the setting.) Ask volunteers to provide other examples. Finally, ask the class to describe what reading tools they can use to understand the various functions of setting in a story.

Teaching Approach

Use of the Handbook

Have a volunteer read aloud the two paragraphs at the top of page 329. Reinforce how setting can shape the plot of a story. Then have students read silently the excerpt from *Cry, the Beloved Country*. Ask students, How does the change in setting affect the plot and mood of the story? What impact does the change have on Stephen Kumalo? Emphasize the importance of close reading and rereading when analyzing time and place. Then familiarize students with visualizing the setting and assessing its importance in a story. Refer them to the discussion of listing key settings and making sketches on pages 330–331.

Extend the Handbook

Have students write a journal entry about how the setting of the story affects the plot. As a class, discuss their thoughts.

Assessment

Ask students:

■ In what ways can the setting of a story influence the plot?

■ How can listing key settings and making sketches help you draw conclusions about setting and its relationship to plot?

WEEK 17

Focus on Characters

For use with *Reader's Handbook* pages 332–344

Daily Lessons	Summary
Lesson 1 **Fictional Characters: An Overview**	Have students recall favorite literary characters and discuss their most memorable qualities. Present an overview of how an author reveals character in a work of fiction.
Lesson 2 **Key Character Terms**	Establish a shared vocabulary of literary terms students can use when discussing characterization.
Lesson 3 **Character and Plot**	Help students understand the relationship between the characters and plot of a story.
Lesson 4 **Character and Theme**	Discuss character and theme. Have students apply what they've learned about theme to Tobias Wolff's "Powder."

Lesson Resources

See *Student Applications Book 10* pages 141–142.

See *Teacher's Guide* pages 211–217.

See *Test Book* for multiple-choice and short-answer tests.

See Website www.greatsource.com/rehand

For more practice, see also *Sourcebook* Grade 10, pages 197–218; *Daybook* Grade 10, pages 103–116

WEEK 18

Focus on Dialogue

For use with *Reader's Handbook* pages 351–358

Daily Lessons	Summary
Lesson 1 **Understanding the Forms of Dialogue**	Reinforce students' understanding of the forms of dialogue and dramatic terms, such as speech tags, extended quotations, and embedded dialogue.
Lesson 2 **Using the Strategy: Close Reading**	Further students' understanding of the strategy of close reading. Help students see the importance of finding and then analyzing key bits of dialogue in a story.
Lesson 3 **Dialogue and Character**	Discuss how writers use dialogue as a way of establishing character.
Lesson 4 **Dialogue, Plot, and Mood**	Help students understand how dialogue can provide background information, emphasize a conflict, and advance a story's plot.

Lesson Resources

See *Student Applications Book 10* pages 146–147.

See *Teacher's Guide* pages 223–227.

See *Test Book* for multiple-choice and short-answer tests.

See Website www.greatsource.com/rehand

For more practice, see also *Sourcebook* Grade 10, pages 73–84; *Daybook* Grade 10, pages 41–45.

WEEK 17
Lesson 1
Fictional Characters: An Overview

For use with *Reader's Handbook* pages 333–334

Goals

In this lesson, students expand their understanding of the purpose of characters and characterization.

Teaching Focus

Background

Characters are the people and animals in works of fiction that drive the story forward. Characterization is the technique authors use to develop the personality of their characters. Good writers establish characters through dialogue, behavior, thoughts, feelings, and interactions with other characters. The purpose of this lesson is to refine students' understanding of character and build knowledge of the techniques of characterization.

Instruction

Engage students in an informal conversation about their favorite literary characters. What were their most memorable qualities? Ask them to describe what made the character stand out. Then ask volunteers to define four terms: *plot, setting, character,* and *characterization*. After hearing their thoughts, define the terms yourself. Finally, ask students to brainstorm ways that authors develop characters and intersperse hints about them throughout a story.

Teaching Approach

Use of the Handbook

Ask a volunteer to read Clues about Characters on page 333 of the handbook. Compare the character clues discussed here with the ones students generated. Then ask students to discuss the five different character clues and what they can reveal. Next, ask students to read about Character Maps on page 334. Have them recall clues about their favorite character and record them in a Character Map.

Extend the Handbook

Divide the class into small groups. Have students discuss their favorite characters and, if they can, list authors who are masters of characterization. Have them describe clues that the author used to bring characters to life. Then come together as a class and discuss the students' list of characters and authors.

Assessment

Ask students:

■ What is the purpose of characters in a work of fiction?

■ What clues does an author use to represent character?

■ What reading tools might help you better understand a character?

126

WEEK 17
Lesson 2
Key Character Terms

For use with *Reader's Handbook* pages 332–337

Goals

In this lesson, students learn terms to describe characters and characterization.

Teaching Focus

Background

Experienced readers use specific literary terms to describe characters and characterization. These terms—which include *protagonist, antagonist,* and *flat* and *round characters*—are a kind of shorthand readers can use when discussing the relative importance of each character in a work.

Instruction

Generally speaking, character terms are easy for students to understand and remember. To review some of these terms, ask students questions about their favorite characters or works of fiction: Is your favorite character one of the most prominent in the work? Then ask: What terms can you use to distinguish between different types of characters? Give students an opportunity to recall as many terms as they can. Then define each of the character terms described in the handbook. Establish characteristics of round and flat characters, protagonists and antagonists, major and minor characters, and static and dynamic characters.

Teaching Approach

Use of the Handbook

Ask a volunteer to read Major and Minor Characters on page 333 of the *Reader's Handbook*. Then ask students to make a Character Map and read silently the excerpts from Guy de Maupassant's "The Necklace" on pages 335, 336, and 337. Discuss the passages as a class. Have students use character terms to describe what they read of "The Necklace."

Extend the Handbook

For their own reference, ask students to list the character terms alphabetically and define each one. Suggest that they provide examples of each type of character as a way of remembering each term and becoming comfortable with using the terms.

Assessment

Ask students:

■ What purpose do key character terms serve?

■ What is the difference between a protagonist and an antagonist?

■ What is the difference between dynamic and static characters?

WEEK 17
Lesson 3
Character and Plot

For use with *Reader's Handbook* pages 338–340

Goals

In this lesson, students explore the mutually dependent relationship between character and plot.

Teaching Focus

Background

Do characters shape the plot or does the plot shape characters? Actually, the two elements are so intertwined that it's impossible to generalize on this question. Just as the main characters affect the plot, so do plot changes affect the characters. This lesson focuses on the interplay between characters and plot and shows students strategies for interpreting the characters and plot in fictional works.

Instruction

Impress upon students the role characters play in the plot of a story or novel. Subtle changes in characters' language, actions, or thoughts can represent or foreshadow developments in the plot. Have students think about their favorite fictional characters again. How does a character's personality and actions move the plot along?

Teaching Approach

Use of the Handbook

Call students' attention to the questions about character and plot on page 338 of the handbook. Ask volunteers to respond to these questions using their favorite character from a novel or story. Ask students, How would the plot change if this character were taken out of the story? Then spend time in discussion to emphasize how indispensable character development is to the action of the story. Next, ask students to read silently the paragraph at the bottom of page 338 and the passage from "The Necklace" on page 339 of the handbook. Have them discuss the passages from "The Necklace" using the questions on page 338. Finally, discuss how the Inference Chart on page 340 can help students discover links between characters and plot.

Extend the Handbook

Ask students to create an Inference Chart for their favorite literary character. Then ask them to write an entry in their journals that discusses ways of analyzing characters and addresses the relationship between character and plot.

Assessment

Ask students:

■ What is the relationship between character and plot in a work of fiction?

■ How can an Inference Chart help in analyzing characters?

128

WEEK 17
Lesson 4

Character and Theme

For use with *Reader's Handbook* pages 340–342

Goals

Here students will discover the relationship between the characters in a work of fiction and its theme.

Teaching Focus

Background

In this lesson, students learn that examining key character details can help them identify and understand the themes of a story. By the end of the lesson, students should understand that what characters say and do can reveal important clues about a story's central theme and the details the author uses to develop it.

Instruction

Begin by asking volunteers to define the literary term *theme*. Reinforce their understanding of the term by explaining that theme is the writer's main point or unifying message in a work of fiction. Familiarize students with two common types of clues that authors use to relay their themes: Characters' Actions, Feelings, or Thoughts about Life and a Change in a Character. Read the description of these clues found on pages 340–341 of the Handbook.

Teaching Approach

Use of the Handbook

Have students read the passages from "The Necklace" on page 342 of the handbook. Have them keep in mind the questions about the changes in characters that appear on page 341. Encourage them to pay attention to Matilda's thoughts and reactions. Discuss students' ideas about the theme of the story. Ask them to suggest other questions that readers can use to figure out the theme of a literary work.

Extend the Handbook

Have students apply what they learned about characters and theme to Tobias Wolff's "Powder," the short story they read in the previous chapter of the handbook (270–275). Have them create a Character Map or Inference Chart to help them keep track of clues about character and theme. When they've finished reading the story and taking notes, ask them questions about the story: What are possible themes of the story? What clues about the father and son in "Powder" point to these themes? If you have time, ask students to record their thoughts about the themes of "Powder" in their journals.

Assessment

Ask students:

■ What is the relationship between character and theme?

■ What steps After Reading can you use to identify the theme of a story?

Understanding the Forms of Dialogue

For use with *Reader's Handbook* pages 351–354

Goals

In this lesson, students review the usual form of dialogue and learn key terms they can use when analyzing a piece of dialogue.

Teaching Focus

Background

In this lesson, you'll review the rules of dialogue—such as that most dialogue is set off by quotation marks and a writer will begin a new paragraph to indicate a new speaker. But not all dialogue in a story is spoken. In many works, the characters think aloud more often than they speak aloud.

Instruction

Begin by asking students to discuss what they know about the correct form of dialogue. Ask for the rules regarding quotation marks, speech tags, and paragraphing. Then list these dialogue terms on the board: *extended quotations, embedded quotations, representative dialogue,* and *internal dialogue.* Have students read the definitions for each and discuss the examples.

Teaching Approach

Use of the Handbook

Read aloud the introductory discussion on the top of page 351. Discuss the main purposes of dialogue: it can provide clues about characters, affect the mood, and explain and advance the plot in a story. Have students explain what they know of the forms of dialogue and ask them to read the notes made for "Blues Ain't No Mockinbird" (page 352). Then have students turn to page 353 and read about extended and embedded quotations. Discuss the characteristics of each. Next, have students read page 354. Again, discuss each type of dialogue listed.

Extend the Handbook

Bring to class texts that contain examples of extended quotations, embedded quotations, representative dialogue, and internal dialogue. Have students identify each type and explain how they know.

Assessment

Ask students:

■ What is the difference between representative and internal dialogue?

■ What is the purpose of speech tags? How can they help you make inferences about the character speaking?

WEEK 18
Lesson 2

Using the Strategy: Close Reading

For use with *Reader's Handbook* page 355

Goals

In this lesson, students review the strategy of close reading and apply what they've learned to reading dialogue.

Teaching Focus

Background

The strategy of close reading is ideal to use when focusing on dialogue because it helps the reader to consider both the denotative and connotative meanings of a character's words. To prevent students from feeling overwhelmed by the amount of text to analyze, however, remind them to focus on key bits of dialogue, rather than try to do a close reading of all the dialogue in a story. Discuss with students how to find key speeches and lines in a work of fiction. Explain that these can provide clues about character and meaning.

Instruction

Remind students that dialogue can offer clues about character, plot, and theme. To find these clues, the reader must read carefully and make inferences. Then discuss the importance of listening to what each character is saying and how he or she is saying it.

Teaching Approach

Use of the Handbook

Ask students to turn to page 355 and begin reading. Have them note the questions in the middle of the page and discuss what they have to do with the dialogue of a story. Point out that the five questions deal with elements of plot, character, and mood. Then have students turn to the discussion of close reading in the Strategy Handbook (pages 714–715) and read these pages carefully. Model for students a close reading of the dialogue from *Cry, the Beloved Country* shown on page 354.

Extend the Handbook

Ask students to choose a dialogue-rich excerpt from a story or novel and then do a close reading of the text. Have them underline clues about character, highlight clues about plot, and circle clues about mood. Ask students, How does this piece of dialogue strengthen your understanding of the story or novel as a whole?

Assessment

Ask students:

■ How can dialogue affect the plot and characters?

■ Why is close reading an effective strategy to use with dialogue?

WEEK 18
Lesson 3
Dialogue and Character

For use with *Reader's Handbook* page 355–356

Goals

Here students learn how to analyze dialogue to find clues about a story's characters.

Teaching Focus

Background

We tend to judge people by what they say and how they say it. Proficient readers do the same when it comes to the characters in a story or novel. What the characters say about themselves and to each other can provide insightful clues about their personalities. Here students will read and respond to two short pieces of dialogue with the intention of making inferences about the speaker.

Instruction

Open your lesson with a question: What can you learn about people from listening to what they say and how they say it? Discuss how the words people use (and often how they pronounce them) can tell us where the person is from, how well he or she was educated, and so on. Then explain that a reader can infer a great deal about a character's motivation and personality by looking for similar clues in the dialogue.

Teaching Approach

Use of the Handbook

Have students work in pairs to read the information under Clues about Character on pages 355–356. Ask students, What is the relationship between character and dialogue in a work of fiction? What inferences can you make about Granddaddy based on what he says and how he says it?

Extend the Handbook

Ask students to write a short explanation of how dialogue can help a reader understand a character's personality. Ask students to use stories or novels from their own reading to substantiate their ideas. When they've finished, have students exchange explanations and make comments on what their partners have written.

For additional practice, ask students to complete pages 146–147 of *Student Applications Book 10*.

Assessment

Ask students:

■ What can dialogue tell you about a story's characters?

■ What reading tool might you use to keep track of your inferences about dialogue and character?

132

WEEK 18
Lesson 4

Dialogue, Plot, and Mood

For use with *Reader's Handbook* pages 357–358

Goals

Here students learn how authors use dialogue to advance the plot and contribute to the mood of the story.

Teaching Focus

Background

In addition to providing clues about character, dialogue can also help a reader better understand the plot and mood of a story. Helping students examine the connection between these literary elements can deepen their understanding of the text.

Instruction

Explain to students that most stories consist of a combination of dialogue and narration. However, readers sometimes rely solely on the narrator for information about what's happening in a story, and thereby miss important plot clues in the characters' dialogue. Ask students, What role can dialogue play in helping readers keep track of the action? What examples can you think of in which the dialogue of the story drives the action? Then discuss mood. Ask students to define the term *mood* and then discuss how what a character says and thinks can set the mood for a story.

Teaching Approach

Use of the Handbook

Have a student volunteer read aloud the information about mood on page 356. Then discuss the mood Bambera creates with these lines from "Blues Ain't No Mockinbird." If students need additional help with mood, have them return to "Powder." See if they can find bits of dialogue that contribute establishing to its mood. Begin your discussion of dialogue and plot. Have students turn to page 357. Ask students, What do these two excerpts reveal about the plot? At the end of the lesson, read aloud page 358. Discuss how a Double-entry Journal can help students reflect upon character.

Extend the Handbook

Have students excerpt two pieces of dialogue from "Powder" that they feel offer clues about mood and plot. Ask them to write the dialogue in the left column of a Double-entry Journal. In the right column, they should respond to the dialogue with their own thoughts and feelings.

Assessment

Ask students:

∎ How can readers use dialogue to understand a story's plot? What about a story's mood?

∎ What is a example of dialogue affecting plot?

WEEK 19
Reading a Novel

For use with *Reader's Handbook* pages 288–312

Daily Lessons	Summary
Lesson 1 **The Novel: An Overview**	Discuss with students characteristics of the genre and the chief challenges it presents.
Lesson 2 **Literary Elements in a Novel**	Review important literary elements in a novel, including point of view, characters, and setting.
Lesson 3 **Literary Elements in a Novel (continued)**	Continue your discussion of literary elements by focusing on plot, theme, and author's style.
Lesson 4 **Before Reading a Novel**	Introduce the novel excerpt presented in the *Reader's Handbook* and discuss how to apply the Before Reading stage of the reading process to novels.

Lesson Resources

Overheads
For this lesson, use:
Overheads 26 and 27: Previewing a Novel

See *Student Applications Book 10* pages 124–136.

See *Teacher's Guide* pages 189–200.

See *Test Book* for multiple-choice and short-answer tests.

See Website www.greatsource.com/rehand

For more practice, see also *Sourcebook* Grade 10, pages 197–218; *Daybook* Grade 10, pages 107–113.

134

WEEK 20

Reading a Novel (continued)

For use with *Reader's Handbook* pages 288–312

Daily Lessons	Summary
Lesson 5 **Reading a Novel**	Discuss the During Reading stage of the reading process and how each step works with a novel. Emphasize the importance of reading with a purpose and using graphic organizers.
Lesson 6 **Using Graphic Organizers**	Reinforce students' understanding of the strategy of using graphic organizers. Explore various organizers that work well with fiction.
Lesson 7 **Connecting to a Novel**	Review the Connect stage of the reading process and the ways in which making a connection can enhance a reader's understanding and enjoyment of a novel.
Lesson 8 **After Reading a Novel**	Help students apply the After Reading stage of the reading process to a novel. Instruct them to use what they've learned to respond to a novel they read on their own.

Lesson Resources

See *Student Applications Book 10* pages 124–136.

See *Teacher's Guide* pages 189–200.

See *Test Book* for multiple-choice and short-answer tests.

See Website www.greatsource.com/rehand

For more practice, see also *Sourcebook* Grade 10, pages 197–218; *Daybook* Grade 10, pages 107–113.

WEEK 19
Lesson 1

The Novel: An Overview

For use with *Reader's Handbook* pages 288–312

Goals

In this lesson, students explore the characteristics of the novel.

Teaching Focus

Background

Of the literary genres, the novel is considered the most important. It is also perhaps the most varied. You can divide the genre into numerous sub-genres, including science fiction, fantasy, historical fiction, horror, romance, and so on—all of which have their own unique characteristics. Use this lesson as your opportunity to offer a brief overview of the characteristics of the novel and what distinguishes it from other literary genres. (Generally, the length, scope, and complexity of the plot make the novel distinct from the short story.) Help students activate prior knowledge about various sub-genres and encourage them to discuss their relative enjoyment of each one.

Instruction

Begin by asking students to brainstorm various types of novels. Discuss distinguishing characteristics of each type and work to get a sense of students' likes and dislikes. Then have students get together in small groups and discuss descriptions they would write for the genre. Examples might include *long, complicated, engaging,* and so on. Finish the lesson by reviewing each group's work.

Teaching Approach

Use of the Handbook

Ask a student volunteer to read aloud the unit opener on page 288. Discuss the three items in the Goals box. Have students think about their goals when they begin to read a novel. Ask students, What do you hope to learn? What is a good reason for reading this novel?

Extend the Handbook

Have students recall a novel they read for a school assignment or during their spare time that they particularly enjoyed. Ask students, What made the book fun to read? What do they remember most about it? Try to get a sense of the type of novel that most appeals to students and help them build a list of novels for outside reading.

Assessment

Ask students:

■ In what ways is a novel different from other literary forms?

■ What is a description of the genre *novel?*

WEEK 19
Lesson 2 # Literary Elements in a Novel

For use with *Reader's Handbook* pages 293–301

Goals

In this lesson, students explore important literary terms associated with novels, such as point of view, characters, and setting.

Teaching Focus

Background

This lesson will be the first of two in which you discuss various literary terms needed to speak knowledgeably about a novel. Here you'll focus on *point of view, setting,* and *character*. In the lesson that follows, you'll explore *plot, theme,* and *style*.

Instruction

Write the following literary terms on the board: *point of view, setting,* and *character*. Have students define each, using the definitions provided in the Elements of Fiction section of the *Reader's Handbook* as needed. Then discuss why a reader needs to recognize the three elements and analyze how they work in every novel they read. Explore the ways in which understanding point of view, setting, and character can heighten a reader's enjoyment of the work while at the same time strengthen their comprehension of the author's central ideas.

Teaching Approach

Use of the Handbook

Begin by pointing out the Fiction Organizer on page 293. Explain that an organizer such as this one can help students keep track of the major literary elements of a work. Then begin your detailed discussion of point of view, setting, and character. Use the information on pages 293–301 in addition to the relevant pages of the Elements of Fiction section of the *Reader's Handbook*.

Extend the Handbook

For additional practice with point of view, setting, and character, have students complete pages 139–142 in *Student Applications Book 10*.

Assessment

Ask students:

■ What is point of view? What are the various types of point of view?

■ How would you define setting? Why should a reader understand the setting when reading a novel?

■ What are some of the methods a novelist might use to establish character?

137

Literary Elements in a Novel (continued)

For use with *Reader's Handbook* pages 302–307

Goals

Here you'll continue your exploration of literary terms by focusing on plot, theme, and style.

Teaching Focus

Background

The theme of a work generally causes students the most trouble. In this lesson, you'll want to carefully review what students have learned about theme. You'll want to do the same for *plot* and *style,* since many readers have a hard time seeing how these individual elements work together and contribute to the effect of the whole.

Instruction

Begin this lesson by writing the three literary elements to be discussed on the board. Then discuss each element in some detail. Introduce such plot terms as *exposition, rising action,* and *climax.* In discussing *theme,* be sure to help students differentiate between the "big idea," or topic, of a work and its theme. End the lesson with an overview of the characteristics of an author's style and how word choice and use of literary elements such as figurative language, imagery, and so on can affect the style of a piece. See if students can suggest writers with distinctive styles, such as Ernest Hemingway, James Joyce, and even Stephen King.

Teaching Approach

Use of the Handbook

Direct students' attention to page 302. Ask them to read silently the information on plot. Have students recall what they learned about Summary Notes during the short story unit. After you finish with *plot,* hold the same types of brief discussions about *theme* and *style.*

Extend the Handbook

For additional practice with plot and theme, have students complete pages 137–138 and 143–144 in *Student Applications Book 10.* Then discuss all six literary elements associated with novels that were discussed in this lesson and the last one.

Assessment

Ask students:

■ What are the five major elements of a plot?

■ How is a novel's theme different from its big ideas?

■ In what ways can an author's style affect your enjoyment of the work?

WEEK 19
Lesson 4

Before Reading a Novel

For use with *Reader's Handbook* pages 288–293

Goals

Here students will review the Before Reading stage of the reading process and see how it applies to a novel.

Teaching Focus

Because most novels are quite long, the Set a Purpose stage of the reading process takes on particular importance. Readers who don't have a clear purpose in mind for reading run the risk of getting lost halfway through the novel, or they have a difficult time recalling important events and elements in the work. Emphasize how important it is to set a purpose that includes learning about point of view, characters, setting, plot, theme, and style.

Instruction

Begin by emphasizing that with understanding comes enjoyment. If a reader understands a character's motivation, then the character and the work as a whole will be more enjoyable and relevant. Point out the purpose questions listed in the *Reader's Handbook*. Ask students to set their own purpose for reading the excerpt from *All Quiet on the Western Front*. Finish by asking students to preview the novel pages in the handbook.

Teaching Approach

Use of the Handbook

Direct the class to read page 289. Read the instructions on how to set a purpose and preview a novel. Also spend a few minutes discussing the Webs on page 290. Ask students, How can a Before Reading Web such as this one prepare you for what's to come? At the end of the lesson, ask students to do their own previews of *All Quiet on the Western Front*. Have them make Webs in their journals.

Extend the Handbook

Ask students to reflect upon the title *All Quiet on the Western Front*. Ask students, What do you think it is about? What might be the setting of the work? What do you think the characters will be like? Have students write their predictions in their reading journals. Then ask them to add to their original predictions after they complete their preview of the text.

Assessment

Ask students:

■ How do the Before Reading steps of the reading process work with novels?

■ What is one tool for helping you preview a novel?

Reading a Novel

For use with *Reader's Handbook* pages 294–303

Goals

In this lesson, students will review the During Reading steps of the reading process and learn how to apply them to a novel.

Teaching Focus

Background

Readers of novels probably have at least six purpose questions prior to reading. They use those questions to help them stay focused and organized as they read. The concept of reading with a purpose in mind is an orienting technique that can help students cope with the complexity and length of a novel.

Instruction

Begin with a review of the work students did at the Plan stage of the reading process. Duplicate on the board the Fiction Organizer shown on page 293 and ask students to create one in their reading journals. Point out the connection between the purpose questions on page 294 and the boxes in the Fiction Organizer.

Teaching Approach

Use of the Handbook

Ask a student volunteer to read aloud the questions on page 294 and then first page of the excerpt (page 295). Pause after the reading and ask: What does the novel seem to be about? and What is the point of view? Model how to use the Fiction Organizer for answers to these and other questions. Then have students work in small groups to read the second, third, and fourth excerpts from the novel (pages 296, 299, and 300). As a group, they should pause after each section of the novel and discuss another literary element on the organizer. Remind the class that they'll be making notes about each of these elements.

Extend the Handbook

Ask students to create a Fiction Organizer for a novel they've read outside of class. Encourage them to use specific quotes from the text where appropriate. Ask various volunteers to report on their work to the rest of the class.

Assessment

Ask students:

■ What does "Read with a Purpose" mean when it comes to novels?

■ Why is it important to keep track of various literary elements as you read?

WEEK 20
Lesson 6
Using Graphic Organizers

For use with *Reader's Handbook* pages 293–306

Goals

In this lesson, students review the strategy of using graphic organizers and then discuss various organizers that work well when reading novels.

Teaching Focus

Background

In this lesson, you'll discuss why the strategy of using graphic organizers is a particularly good one to use with novels. Explain that novels can be quite different. Some have long, complex plots. Other involve in-depth studies of one or more characters. Because novels are so varied, they demand a versatile, flexible strategy such as using graphic organizers.

Instruction

Ask students to think of organizers they currently use when reading novels. Lead them to a review of important organizers shown in the Reading Tools section, including Character Map, Story String, Theme Diagram, and so on. Discuss the purpose of each one. End with a general discussion of the strategy of using graphic organizers and the reasons it is so appropriate for novels.

Teaching Approach

Use of the Handbook

Choose an organizer from the Reading Tools section of the handbook that you'd like students to use with the novel. For example, you might suggest a Character Map or a Plot Diagram. Ask students to record what they know and present their ideas to a small group. Try through these small groups to introduce 3 or 4 different organizers.

Extend the Handbook

Ask small groups of students to research information on Erich Remarque. Have them hunt for specific information about *All Quiet on the Western Front,* including reviews, critical response, and so on. After they've finished researching, have the group present what they've found to the rest of the class.

Assessment

Ask students:

■ How can the strategy of using graphic organizers make it easier to understand—and respond to—a novel?

■ Which graphic organizers works best for plot?

■ Which ones work best for characters?

Connecting with a Novel

For use with *Reader's Handbook* pages 308

Goals

In this lesson, students will discuss the importance of making a personal connection to the people, places, and events described in a novel.

Teaching Focus

Background

Active readers know that making a personal connection to what they read can help them better understand the central ideas of the work. Connecting takes on a particular importance when reading a novel because of the length and complexity of most novels. A personal connection to a novel helps sustain the interest in reading.

Instruction

Begin by reviewing with students what it means to "connect" to a text. Discuss the purpose of making connections and the types of questions readers might ask themselves to facilitate the process. These include "What do I think of these characters?" and "What does this remind me of from my own life?" Model for students how to make connection notes on sticky notes as they read. Direct students also to the Make Connection chart on page 748 and model how it can be applied to the novel.

Teaching Approach

Use of the Handbook

Ask a volunteer to read aloud the first paragraph on page 308. Point out the five Connect questions in the middle of the page. Ask students, What are some other Connect questions that you might ask yourself? Then have students make their own connections to the paragraph from Remarque's novel. Finish the lesson by modeling use of the Making Connections Chart shown on page 748. Discuss the purpose of the organizer and how it can be used with a novel.

Extend the Handbook

Ask students to create a Making Connections Chart and use it with the novel they've been reading. Invite students to present their work in small groups.

Assessment

Ask students:

■ What does it mean to "connect" with a novel?

■ How can making connections help you read more actively?

■ What kinds of questions should you ask when making connections to a novel?

142

WEEK 20
Lesson 8

After Reading a Novel

For use with *Reader's Handbook* pages 309–312

Goals

Here students will explore the After Reading stage of the reading process with a novel. In addition, students will review synthesizing as a rereading strategy.

Teaching Focus

Background

Students need to learn the importance of reflecting upon what they've read. The easiest way to do this is to return to the original reading purpose questions and check to see if they have accomplished what they set out to do. If they haven't met their purpose, or if they're a bit unsure of how one or more of the literary elements work in a novel, they'll need to do some rereading. Point out that the rereading strategy of synthesizing can help them pull together elements of a novel and see it as an artistic whole.

Instruction

Open with a review of the steps of the After Reading stage of the reading process and the importance of pausing and reflecting. Then have students return to the Fiction Organizers they created for Remarque's novel. Ask them to fill in gaps as needed, especially in the "theme" section of the organizer. Point out the six Looking Back questions on page 309. Help students link these questions to their original purpose questions (page 294) that they began with when they started reading.

Teaching Approach

Use of the Handbook

Have students work in pairs to read pages 309–311. When they've finished, discuss the rereading strategy of synthesizing. Point out the Fiction Organizer on page 310 and ask students to consider their own ideas about *All Quiet on the Western Front*. Finish by having students read about ways to remember a novel (page 312).

Extend the Handbook

Invite students to apply the After Reading stage of the reading process to the novel they've been reading outside of class. As a final activity, have them write in their reading journals a summary of the novel's plot and a short analysis of one literary element.

Assessment

Ask students:

■ How can the After Reading stage of the reading process help you process what you've read in a novel?

■ What is synthesizing and how does it work as an After Reading strategy?

WEEK 21
Focus on Theme

For use with *Reader's Handbook* pages 345–350

Daily Lessons	Summary
Lesson 1 **Identifying the Central Topics**	Activate students' prior knowledge of theme. Discuss techniques they can use to identify the central topics of a story.
Lesson 2 **Connecting Characters to the Central Topics**	Explore the relationship between the characters and central topics in a work of fiction.
Lesson 3 **Writing a Theme Statement**	Model for students how to write an insightful, clearly worded theme statement.
Lesson 4 **Gathering Supporting Details**	Stress the importance of substantiating inferences about theme with details from the story.

Lesson Resources

See *Student Applications Book 10* pages 143–145.

See *Teacher's Guide* pages 218–222.

See *Test Book* for multiple-choice and short-answer tests.

See Website www.greatsource.com/rehand

For more practice, see also *Daybook* Grade 10, pages 122–125.

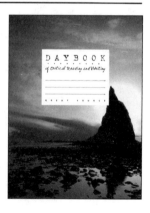

WEEK 22
Elements of Poetry

For use with *Reader's Handbook* pages 423–443

Daily Lessons	Summary
Lesson 1 **Elements of Poetry:** **An Overview**	Have students skim this section of the handbook, noting familiar and unfamiliar elements of poetry. Use their responses to plan the lessons that follow.
Lesson 2 **Figurative Language**	Explore with students figurative language and the effect its use can have on the meaning of a poem.
Lesson 3 **Poetic Devices**	Discuss *rhyme, rhythm,* and *repetition* in poetry. Review other "sound" elements students might encounter when reading verse.
Lesson 4 **Types of Poetry: Free** **Verse and Lyric Poetry**	Build background about two types of poetry: free verse and lyric. Have students apply what they've learned by assigning them to read a poem outside of class.

Lesson Resources

See *Teacher's Guide* pages 233–249.

See Website www.greatsource.com/rehand

See *Test Book* for multiple-choice and short-answer tests.

For more practice, see also *Sourcebook* Grade 10, pages 66–72; *Daybook* Grade 10, pages 169–204.

WEEK 21
Lesson 1 Identifying Central Topics

For use with *Reader's Handbook* pages 345–346

Goals

Here students activate prior knowledge of theme and discuss techniques for finding the central topics of a work.

Teaching Focus

Background

Good stories and novels do more than simply entertain; they provide fresh ways for readers to reflect upon familiar issues or ideas. Themes are the series of thoughts and ideas about life that hold a work together. They are the literary element that can turn a well-told story into a masterwork. In this unit, you'll explore the importance of making inferences about theme when reading fiction.

Instruction

Before doing anything else, make the point that a reader must identify the central topics of a story or novel before he or she can interpret the theme. Identifying the central topics is simply a matter of asking oneself, "What is the story mostly about?"

Teaching Approach

Use of the Handbook

Ask a student to read aloud the unit opener on page 345. Encourage the class to reflect on both the goals of the unit and their own goals for learning about theme. Then engage students in a whole-class discussion of the handbook's definition of theme and how theme differs from the central topic of the work. Next, have students turn to the three-step Plan for Understanding Theme on page 346. Last, concentrate on completing Step 1. Have students read independently the information about finding the central topics in a work. Then come together as a class and discuss central topics in Remarque's novel.

Extend the Handbook

Divide the class into groups of three. Have each group take one column of topics from the Common Topics for Themes list on page 346 and develop a bibliography of short stories and novels that explore these topics. Challenge students to think of three or more works for each topic.

Assessment

Ask students:

■ What is the first step in identifying the theme?

■ What is the difference between a topic and a theme?

Connecting Characters to the Central Topics

For use with *Reader's Handbook* page 347

Goals

In this lesson, students develop an understanding of how character details can provide clues about the themes.

Teaching Focus

Background

After readers identify the central topics in a work (and perhaps whittle their list down to the two or three most important), they can begin the process of making inferences about theme. Good readers know that a character's words, thoughts, and actions can provide clues about theme. In addition, changes in a character's feelings about himself or herself—and about life in general—also can signal theme.

Instruction

Explain to students that, after they find the central topics of a work, they should begin thinking about what the characters do and say that relate to the central topics. To illustrate your point, share an example from a story or novel students know well. Be sure students understand that a graphic organizer, such as a Summary Notes, can help students explore a character's connection to the central topics.

Teaching Approach

Use of the Handbook

Have students work in pairs to read and discuss page 347 of the *Reader's Handbook*. Point out key information appearing under Step 2, especially the list of "clues" readers can examine when considering the central topics and themes of a work. Remind the class that character connections to topic and theme should appear throughout the work. If students can't find enough details to support a particular topic, they should begin again with another topic.

Extend the Handbook

Give students additional practice using the graphic organizers shown in the Reading Tools section of the handbook. To that end, you might want to invite them to create a Fiction Organizer for a novel or story they've read this year in class. Be sure they make notes about the central topics and/or themes.

Assessment

Ask students:

■ How can analyzing characters help readers identify a story's theme?

■ What are four clues about theme should you look for in a story?

WEEK 21
Lesson 3 — Writing a Theme Statement

For use with *Reader's Handbook* pages 349–350

Goals

Here students will learn how take a central topic in a work and develop a clear, effective theme statement that can be substantiated with evidence from the story.

Teaching Focus

Background

Step 3 of the Plan for Understanding Theme involves putting into words what the author is trying to say about life through his or her central topics. In this lesson, students will learn not only how to recognize a story's theme, but also how to articulate that theme effectively.

Instruction

Theme is the statement about life that the author wants to convey about the topic. Explain that, after reading, students can use the clues they found throughout the story to help them develop a theme statement. Then write this equation on the board:

Central topic + What the author says about it = The author's theme

Using the theme equation with the Topic and Theme Organizer on page 349 of the *Reader's Handbook* should make the task of inferring theme very logical.

Teaching Approach

Use of the Handbook

Work with students as they read the strategies for developing theme statements on pages 349–350. Spend the majority of the class period walking them through the sample Topic and Theme Organizer. Point out that the organizer begins with a central topic and includes three or more character clues about that central topic (see Step 2). In the star, students write what the author is trying to teach readers about life.

Extend the Handbook

Have students think about what they've learned thus far about theme. Ask them to make a list of questions and comments they have about central topics and themes. Then discuss the qualities of a good theme statement and have students write a description in their reading journals.

Assessment

Ask students:

■ What is the relationship between a story's central topic and its theme?

■ How can you determine a story's theme?

■ How is a stated theme different from an implied theme?

148

WEEK 21
Lesson 4

Gathering Supporting Details

For use with *Reader's Handbook* pages 345–350

Goals

Here students will learn the importance of finding details from the work that support their theme statement.

Teaching Focus

Background

Without realizing it, readers call upon their prior knowledge and personal experiences when making inferences about theme. This means that different readers will make different inferences about the same story's central topics and themes. What students need to understand, then, is that any interpretation of theme a reader offers can be valid so long as it is supported by details from the story.

Instruction

Review with students the Plan for Understanding Theme. Then explain that after they complete Step 3, students need to check to be sure that the theme statement they've written can be substantiated with details from the story. Supporting details can relate to the characters, dialogue, setting, plot, or even style.

Teaching Approach

Use of the Handbook

Point out to students that the Topic and Theme Organizer on page 349 has three spaces for them to add support for their theme, but they can add many more details in support of a theme. To show that a theme is pervasive, encourage students to offer different kinds of support, such as changes in a character, dialogue, and events in the plot that all point to the theme.

Extend the Handbook

For additional practice with theme, have students complete pages 143–145 of *Student Applications Book 10*.

Assessment

Ask students:

■ Why do different readers have different ideas about a story's theme?

■ Where in the story should you look for details that support the theme?

■ How has this lesson changed your attitude about making theme inferences as you read?

Elements of Poetry: An Overview

For use with *Reader's Handbook* pages 423–443

Goals

In this lesson, students receive an introduction to common characteristics of poems.

Teaching Focus

Background

This lesson and the three that follow offer you the opportunity to play a role in turning high school students into devotees of poetry. Specifically, you can use this unit to familiarize students with the techniques and styles that poets use, and then teach them effective ways to read and interpret poetry.

Instruction

Explain that this week will familiarize students with various techniques and styles poets use. After they finish this unit, students can use it as a reference tool for the next unit, Reading Poetry (pages 388–422). Begin your instruction by asking students to name poetic elements they remember. Write their responses on the board, and have them define the terms as best they can.

Teaching Approach

Use of the Handbook

Have students look at the list of terms on page 423 of the *Reader's Handbook*. Call their attention to any terms that they may not have mentioned or don't know how to define. Then turn to the appropriate page in the handbook and have volunteers read the definition. In this way, students become familiar with some of the terms and gain practice using the Elements section as a reading tool. Help students categorize the different elements. For example, explain that alliteration, consonance, onomatopoeia, and rhythm are all elements that poets use to manipulate the sound of a poem.

Extend the Handbook

Ask students to choose one of the techniques or styles from the list on page 423 and read about it on the appropriate page of the handbook. Then have them either write phrases or lines that illustrate the meaning of the term, or find an example of it in their textbook.

Assessment

Ask students:

■ What are 3 or 4 elements of poetry and what do they mean?

■ How can knowing elements of poetry help you read it?

WEEK 22
Lesson 2 — Figurative Language

For use with *Reader's Handbook* pages 425, 427, 429–430, 433–434, 436, 440, 442

Goals

In this lesson, students learn about several devices that poets use to enrich the language of their poems.

Teaching Focus

Background

A poem is like a rose in full bloom. Each petal is beautiful in its own right, but the combined effect of layers of petals is majestic. Metaphors, similes, and various forms of symbolism are the "petals" of a poem. They give meaning to the work and stimulate readers' emotions and imaginations. In this lesson, students will learn about the styles and techniques poets use to transform a group of relatively simple words into a profound and resonant work of art.

Instruction

Give students an overview of the figurative and symbolic elements of poetry, stressing that poets use these elements to give their poems meaning and depth. Explain that figurative language often involves likening or identifying one thing with another. Metaphors and similes are common devices for saying that one thing resembles another. Students should understand that because poems are so short, poets have to use each word judiciously. Figurative language helps them achieve maximum meaning with minimal words. Explain that, in addition to metaphors and similes, this unit will expose students to these common figures of speech: allusion, hyperbole, personification, imagery, and symbols.

Teaching Approach

Use of the Handbook

Many students will be familiar with similes and metaphors. Distinguish metaphors from similes by explaining that metaphors, in effect, equate two disparate things while similes compare two unlike things using the words *like* or *as*. Then divide students into groups and assign each group one or two figures of speech to read about. When everyone is finished, have volunteers from each group summarize its terms.

Extend the Handbook

Have students reread Eve Merriam's poem "Metaphor." Ask them to think of other metaphors for *morning*. If they can't think of any, have them write a journal entry about how Merriam uses metaphor to help us see a new day in a different way.

Assessment

Ask students:

■ What is the difference between a simile and a metaphor?

■ How would you describe what figurative language is?

Poetic Devices

For use with *Reader's Handbook* pages 424, 426, 431, 435, 437–439

Goals

In this lesson, students explore elements that affect the sound and cadence of poetry.

Teaching Focus

Background

Rhythm, rhyme, and repetition lend a musical quality to poetry. These elements can make words dance on the page and sing when read aloud. They also can echo the meaning and contribute to the mood of a poem. In this lesson, you'll help students appreciate the effect of such elements as consonance, alliteration, and onomatopoeia by having them study examples of the concepts and hear how the poems sound when read.

Instruction

Explain that of all the poetic elements rhythm, rhyme, and repetition most directly affect the way poetry sounds when it's read aloud. Rhythm is the pattern of stressed and unstressed syllables that give poems a musical quality. Poets also use changes in the rhythm of a poem to focus readers' attention on a particular word or line. The elements that contribute to the rhythm of a poem are rhyme scheme and inversion. Rhyme, alliteration, and consonance involve the repetition of consonant sounds. Onomatopoeia is another device that affects the sound of poems.

Teaching Approach

Use of the Handbook

Have students read the discussion of repetition, rhyme, and rhythm on pages 437–439. Then have them read about alliteration (page 424), consonance (page 426), inversion (page 431) and onomatopoeia (page 435). Discuss these poetic devices as a class. Stress that alliteration, consonance and inversion can emphasize certain words and provide clues about the meaning of poems, while onomatopoeia enlivens the sound of poems.

Extend the Handbook

Have volunteers read aloud the examples of alliteration, consonance, inversion, and onomatopoeia. Then ask students to write a short journal entry about how these devices can affect the sound of a poem.

Assessment

Ask students:

■ What affect do rhyme, rhythm, and repetition have on the sound of a poem?

■ How can sound elements in poetry contribute to the meaning of a poem?

WEEK 22
Lesson 4

Types of Poetry: Free Verse and Lyric Poetry

For use with *Reader's Handbook* pages 428, 432

Goals

This lesson exposes students to the forms and sounds of free verse and lyric poetry.

Teaching Focus

Background

Most poems typically fall into two broad categories: lyric and free verse. Lyric poetry incorporates elements of rhythm and rhyme to express the poet's thoughts and feelings in a musical way. Odes, haiku, and elegies are some of the many examples of lyric poetry. Free verse, on the other hand, does not follow a regular rhyme scheme, meter, or structure. Poems written in free verse also tend to ignore conventions of capitalization and punctuation.

Instruction

Discuss lyric and free verse with students. Explain that lyric poetry includes many of the elements of rhythm and rhyme that they've learned about in this unit. In contrast, free verse mimics everyday speech, with no set pattern of stressed syllables, no rhymes, and varying line lengths.

Teaching Approach

Use of the Handbook

Have a volunteer read the example of free verse—Frances Chung's "they want me to settle down," on page 428—and the example of lyric—Walt Whitman's "When I heard the Learn'd Astronomer" on page 432. Ask students to discuss how these two forms create two vastly different moods. Lead them to see that free verse has a conversational feel, while the melody and rhythm of lyric poetry creates a more unified impression. Then have students read the descriptions and definitions of both terms. Finally, have students read various other sample poems in the Reading Poetry unit and point out examples of free verse and lyric.

Extend the Handbook

Have students find a poem in their textbook or in an anthology of poems. Ask them to read the poem and identify the type of verse as lyric or free. Then have them write a journal entry about how the various elements contributed to the meaning and mood of the poem.

Assessment

Ask students:

■ What is the difference between free verse and lyric poetry?

■ What is characteristic of lyric poetry? of free verse?

WEEK 23
Reading a Poem

For use with *Reader's Handbook* pages 388–399

Daily Lessons	Summary
Lesson 1 **Reading Poetry: An Overview**	Discuss with students the importance of doing several careful readings of a single poem. Provide an overview of the purpose of each.
Lesson 2 **Reading for Enjoyment and Meaning**	Explore the importance of reading a poem once through without stopping. Explain that the first and second reading of a poem can give readers important clues about the meaning of the work.
Lesson 3 **Reading for Structure and Language**	Consider the role structure plays in poetry. Work with students as they examine the organization and language in Elizabeth Barrett Browning's "Sonnet 43."
Lesson 4 **Reading for Mood and Feeling**	Activate prior knowledge of the literary term *mood* and how to make inferences about the mood of a poem. Finish by guiding students to apply the After Reading stage of the reading process to poetry.

Lesson Resources

Overheads

For this lesson, use:
Overhead 28: Previewing a Poem

See *Student Applications Book 10* pages 150–156.

See *Teacher's Guide* pages 251–259.

See *Test Book* for short-answer and multiple-choice tests.

See Website www.greatsource.com/rehand

For more practice, see also *Sourcebook* Grade 10, pages 82–86; *Daybook* Grade 10, pages 9–20, 21–24, 42–45, 51–52, 183–192, 193–198.

WEEK 24
Focus on Meaning

For use with *Reader's Handbook* pages 408–414

Daily Lessons	Summary
Lesson 1 **Reading for Meaning**	Present an overview of a four-step plan for reading poetry. Discuss the importance of reading for meaning.
Lesson 2 **Using the Strategy: Close Reading**	Assess students' understanding of the strategy and how to use it. Work with students as they do a close reading of "Ex-Basketball Player."
Lesson 3 **Understanding Connotation, Denotation, and Poetic Style**	Discuss connotation, denotation, and poetic style and the effect they can have on a reader's interpretation of a poem.
Lesson 4 **Listening to Your Own Feelings**	Review the importance of making a personal connection to a poem.

Lesson Resources

See *Student Applications Book 10* pages 160–161.

See *Teacher's Guide* page 265–268.

See *Test Book* for multiple-choice and short-answer tests.

See Website www.greatsource.com/rehand

For more practice, see also *Sourcebook* Grade 10, pages 82–86; *Daybook* Grade 10, pages 9–20, 21–24, 42–45, 51–52, 183–192, 193–198.

Reading Poetry: An Overview

For use with *Reader's Handbook* pages 389–392

Goals

This lesson familiarizes students with a five-part plan to use when reading poetry.

Teaching Focus

Background

Many readers—especially student readers—are ambivalent about poetry. They know they're supposed to appreciate its beauty and want to enjoy reading it, but they find the compressed format, figurative language, and heightened vocabulary of poetry too difficult. This lesson teaches students several useful strategies for reading poems. By doing five separate readings of a poem—and concentrating on five separate purposes—students can find poetry more meaningful and more pleasurable.

Instruction

Ask students to write a journal entry about their experiences with poetry. Suggest that they address what they like and dislike about reading poetry. Discuss students' reflections as a class. Then ask how they think they might adapt the reading process to poetry. Explain that it is crucial to read a poem multiple times in order to assimilate all of its elements. Acquaint students with the handbook's plan of doing five careful readings of a poem and explain the purpose of each reading.

Teaching Approach

Use of the Handbook

Have students read pages 389–391. Ask a volunteer to read aloud the description of the Close Reading strategy on page 392 and study the Double-entry Journal as a class. Direct students to do their first careful reading of Elizabeth Barrett Browning's "Sonnet 43." Ask them to reflect in their journals on Browning's sonnet. Ask students, What did they enjoy about this first reading? What questions do they have?

Extend the Handbook

Ask students to choose a poem to study on their own throughout this unit. Before they begin by previewing the poem, remind them to pay attention to the elements listed in the Preview Checklist on page 390. Then have them create a Double-entry Journal and write, in the left column, any words and phrases that captured their attention. Explain that they will interpret these words and phrases later.

Assessment

Ask students:

■ What are the Before Reading steps for poetry?

■ Why would you read a poem a number of times?

WEEK 23

Lesson 2

Reading for Enjoyment and Meaning

For use with *Reader's Handbook* pages 391, 393–394

Goals

In this lesson, students learn how to read a poem for enjoyment as well as meaning.

Teaching Focus

Background

Students might wonder how they can enjoy the first reading of a poem if they don't understand it. Although it seems odd, proficient readers know that a first reading offers the opportunity to enjoy and become familiar with a poem. It can relax readers and put them in the right frame of mind for the more arduous task of interpreting the poem's meaning. In this lesson, students learn more details about the first and second reading of a poem and how a Double-entry Journal can help.

Instruction

Have students recall their first reading of "Sonnet 43." Ask them, What was your first impression of the sonnet? What feelings did it conjure in you? Then discuss the goals of the first and second readings of a poem. During the first reading, students should read the poem slowly and think about their overall reaction to it. Advise them to use a Double-entry Journal for recording their thoughts. During the second reading, they can tackle the meaning of the poem. Tell them that responding to individual words and lines in their own words is a good strategy for inferring a poem's meaning. Stress the usefulness of a Double-entry Journal for this purpose.

Teaching Approach

Use of the Handbook

Walk students through Read with a Purpose on page 393 to reinforce your discussion about first and second readings. Then have students create a Double-entry Journal and read "Sonnet 43" a second time. Tell them to use the strategy of close reading to find clues about the poem's meaning. In the organizer's left column, have them copy an important line that seems to hold clues about the poem's meaning; in the right column, have them paraphrase the line.

Extend the Handbook

Ask students to return to the Double-entry Journal they created in the first lesson. Have them write in the left column their interpretations of the words and phrases they recorded on the right. What can they learn about the meaning of the poem?

Assessment

Ask students:

■ What is the role of the first and second readings of a poem?

■ What reading tools can help you interpret a poem?

WEEK 23
Lesson 3

Reading for Structure and Language

For use with *Reader's Handbook* pages 391, 394–395

Goals

This lesson demonstrates to students that examining structure and language during the third reading of a poem can provide clues about its meaning.

Teaching Focus

Background

Poets choose and arrange words deliberately to create a specific emotional response. The meaning, sound, and rhythm of a poem capture the reader's imagination and offer clues about the poet's intent. Likewise, every detail of a poem's structure matters, from its typography and punctuation to its meter and rhyme. In this lesson, students will learn about the structure of a particular kind of poem—the sonnet—and explore how structure and language can reflect meaning.

Teaching Approach

Instruction

Explain the elements that make up the structure of a poem, including layout, typography, punctuation, rhyme pattern, and the freedom of syntax. Point out that the structure determines the appearance of poems on the page and contributes to how poems sound when they're recited. Have students read "Sonnet 43" a third time with an eye toward its structure and language. Ask them, What do you notice about Browning's word choice? What figures of speech do you notice?

Use of the Handbook

Discuss with students rhyme scheme (the repetition of sounds at the end of lines), and meter (the pattern of syllables within a poem's lines). Explain that sonnets follow a rhythm called *iambic pentameter*. Then have students read pages 394 and 395. Compare their observations about the structure and language of "Sonnet 43" with the Journal Entry on page 394. Explain to students that the entry should serve as a model for evaluating structure and language.

Extend the Handbook

Ask students to return to the poem they've been analyzing in this unit. Have them write a journal entry about the structure and language of the poem. Suggest that they refer to their Double-entry Journals. Ask: *Do you see a connection between the structure and language of the poem and its meaning?*

Assessment

Ask students:

■ What elements make up the structure of a poem?

■ What should you look for in a poem's structure and language?

WEEK 23
Lesson 4

Reading for Mood and Feeling

For use with *Reader's Handbook* pages 391, 396–399

Goals

Here students learn how to read the mood and tone of a poem.

Teaching Focus

Background

Of all the readings of a poem, the fourth reading—during which readers assess mood and feeling—offers students the chance to make the strongest connection to a poem. During this reading, students filter the poem through their own unique lens. Proficient readers also use the fourth reading to evaluate the poet's tone, or attitude toward the subject or reader. This lesson encourages students to trust their instincts when exploring a poem's mood.

Instruction

Write the words *mood* and *tone* on the board. Ask volunteers to define each. Then explain that words or phrases that express emotion offer clues about mood and tone. After having students read page 396, ask them to concentrate on finding clues about mood and tone in "Sonnet 43." Then have them write a journal entry about how the sonnet makes them feel. What were they able to infer about the poem's mood and tone? Discuss students' impressions as a class.

Teaching Approach

Use of the Handbook

Have students read pages 397–399. Then have them read Browning's poem a final time. Emphasize that a fifth reading offers a chance to connect to the poem and appreciate how its elements work together. Invite them to write a journal entry about how "Sonnet 43" relates to their experience. When students finish writing, divide them into small groups and have them walk through the After Reading steps. Suggest that they discuss the poem using the Looking Back questions on page 398 as a guide. Then they can work together to create a Paraphrase Chart.

Extend the Handbook

Ask students to write a letter or email message about "Sonnet 43." Encourage them to describe what they found most striking about the poem. Explain that expressing their reactions will help them commit the poem to memory.

Assessment

Ask students:

■ Why are the tone and mood of a poem important?

■ Why should readers consider their own response to a poem?

WEEK 24
Lesson 1
Reading for Meaning

For use with *Reader's Handbook* pages 408–414

Goals

Here students deepen their understanding of how to find meaning in a poem.

Teaching Focus

Background

Students have learned to use the second reading of a poem to evaluate meaning and the third reading to examine structure and language. In this lesson, they'll become familiar with a four-step plan for finding meaning in a poem by interrogating its language. Each of the steps involve students focusing intensely on one aspect of language, examining single words and phrases, and then assessing how individual words coalesce to bring meaning to a poem.

Instruction

Walk through the four-step plan with students. You might want to list briefly the steps on the board. Step 1 involves evaluating the denotations and connotations of words. The second step requires focusing on elements of poetic style, such as the use of figurative language, imagery, and rhythm. Step 3 is to decipher the poet's tone, or attitude toward the subject, and what mood the poet seeks to create. Step 4 entails readers coming to terms with their own feelings about a poem. Provide an overview of how to implement these steps as part of the reading process for poetry.

Teaching Approach

Use of the Handbook

Explain that students can preview a poem with the four-step plan in mind. While scanning a poem, they should do a cursory search for each use of language. Have students preview John Updike's poem "Ex-Basketball Player" on page 409 of the *Reader's Handbook*. Ask them to make brief notes on what they noticed about Updike's use of language. They will learn definitions of such key concepts as metaphor and connotation in the next three lessons. What's important here is that they note words and phrases that jump out.

Extend the Handbook

Divide students into groups and have them set a purpose based on their preview of "Ex-Basketball Player." The four-step plan provides a basic framework for how they will proceed. But they can note their initial impressions of the poem's meaning and discuss what they will focus on during each step. Have a member of each group summarize the purpose they devised.

Assessment

Ask students:

■ What are the four steps for examining the language of a poem for meaning?

■ What reading tools might work with this plan?

WEEK 24
Lesson 2

Using the Strategy: Close Reading

For use with *Reader's Handbook* pages 409–410

Goals

In this lesson, students become adept at using the strategy of close reading to explore the language of poems.

Teaching Focus

Background

Understanding language is arguably the most important task of reading a poem. The strategy of close reading enables students to focus on the language of a poem and give each word the attention it demands. Here students will learn the best way to do a close reading of a poem.

Instruction

Have students recall the close reading strategy from previous lessons. Explain that conducting a close reading of a poem involves looking at each word on its own terms and then evaluating how it relates to the whole poem. Then mention that Double-entry Journals can help students focus their attention on specific words and phrases. Remind them to use the left column for recording words and phrases.

Teaching Approach

Use of the Handbook

Ask students to do a close reading of "Ex-Basketball Player." Suggest that they record on a Double-entry Journal words that struck them and words that confused them. Furnish students with dictionaries and ask them to define the words they listed in their journals. Reinforce the importance of writing down all of the meanings of a word in the right column of their Double-entry Journals. Familiarize students with the difference between denotations and connotations.

Extend the Handbook

Have students practice using close reading to explore language in a poem of their own choosing. Encourage them to use a Double-entry Journal to record their ideas. For more practice with Double-entry Journals, students can consult page 743 of the *Reader's Handbook*.

Assessment

Ask students:

■ In what ways can close reading help you understand the language of a poem?

■ Why is it important to keep a dictionary handy while reading poetry?

WEEK 24
Lesson 3

Understanding Connotation, Denotation, and Poetic Style

For use with *Reader's Handbook* pages 409, 411–412

Goals

In this lesson, students will learn how to extract the meaning of a poem by examining specific features of its language.

Teaching Focus

Background

Poets use words literally. But they also strive to convey something in the meaning of a word besides what it denotes. The multiple meanings of individual words deepen the meaning of the poem as a whole. Here you will help students unlock the meaning of poems by teaching them how to examine a poet's language and style.

Instruction

Remind students that in the last lesson, they learned the importance of using a dictionary while reading poetry. Here they will discover how to probe the meaning of words even deeper than their dictionary definition. Ask a volunteer to explain the difference between denotation and connotation. Suggest that students also use Double-entry Journals for noting the connotations of words. Then discuss similes, metaphors, and symbols. Students should understand that figurative language adds yet another layer of meaning to a poem. Help them understand how imagery, figurative language, rhythm, and other poetic styles contribute to a poem's meaning.

Teaching Approach

Use of the Handbook

Have students do another close reading of "Ex-Basketball Player." Explain that you want them to pay attention to the connotations of words and the use of figurative language and poetic styles. As they read, ask them to fill in the left column of a Double-entry Journal with examples of figurative language or imagery. Then have them examine the different connotations of words and think about the meaning of imagery and symbols.

Extend the Handbook

Have students read "Ex-Basketball Player" again and write a journal entry that explores the tone and mood of the poem.

Assessment

■ What is the difference between a word's denotation and connotation?

■ How does the language of a poem contribute to its tone and mood?

WEEK 24
Lesson 4

Listening to Your Own Feelings

For use with *Reader's Handbook* pages 409, 413–414

Goals

This lesson encourages students to get in touch with their feelings about a poem during the After Reading stage of the reading process.

Teaching Focus

Background

Whatever emotions poets seek to stir in their audience, readers necessarily come away with their own specific feelings about poems. Students should understand that the personal meaning that they draw from a poem is just as valid as a poet's intended meaning. In this lesson, students learn to use the After Reading stage for poetry as an opportunity to recognize the meaning that they bring to a poem.

Instruction

If you feel students need the review, discuss the components of the After Reading stage of the reading process. Explain that reflecting on a poem after reading can help students clarify its meaning. Underscore the importance of students trusting their own feelings about the meaning of a poem.

Teaching Approach

Use of the Handbook

Have students read the text under the Step 3 heading on page 413 and respond to the questions in the second paragraph. Then have them spend time rereading "Ex-Basketball Player." Encourage them to use the dictionary and reconsider the use of figurative language and imagery.

Extend the Handbook

Give students the option of either writing a journal entry about what "Ex-Basketball Player" means to them or writing their own poem in the style of "Ex-Basketball Player." Whichever exercise they choose, encourage students not to be afraid to express their own opinions and unique interpretations of the poem.

Assessment

Ask students:

∎ What should you do after reading a poem to help you better understand its meaning?

∎ How can writing your own poem or writing about a poem help you understand the meaning of a poem?

WEEK 25
Focus on Sound and Structure

For use with *Reader's Handbook* pages 415–422

Daily Lessons	Summary
Lesson 1 **Organization of Lines**	Introduce concepts of sound and structure in poetry. Discuss characteristics of poetic organization.
Lesson 2 **Repetition**	Analyze types of repetition commonly used in poetry.
Lesson 3 **Sound Devices**	Build understanding of the importance of sound devices.
Lesson 4 **Meter**	Activate prior knowledge of meter. Teach students to differentiate between stressed and unstressed syllables in a line of poetry.

Lesson Resources

See *Student Applications Book 10* pages 162–164.

See *Teacher's Guide* pages 269–273.

See *Test Book* for multiple-choice and short-answer tests.

See Website www.greatsource.com/rehand

For more practice, see also *Sourcebook* Grade 10, pages 82–86; *Daybook* Grade 10, pages 9–20, 21–24, 42–45, 51–52, 183–192 193–198.

WEEK 26
Reading a Play

For use with *Reader's Handbook* pages 446–468

Daily Lessons	Summary
Lesson 1 **Before Reading a Play**	Work with students to apply various Before Reading strategies to a play.
Lesson 2 **Reading with a Purpose**	Help students use During Reading strategies to explore character and plot in a dramatic work.
Lesson 3 **After Reading a Play**	Discuss with students After Reading strategies to use with drama. Offer instruction on the rereading strategy of visualizing and thinking aloud.
Lesson 4 **Elements of Drama**	Walk through the Elements of Drama section with students. Clear up any confusion about key dramatic terms.

Lesson Resources

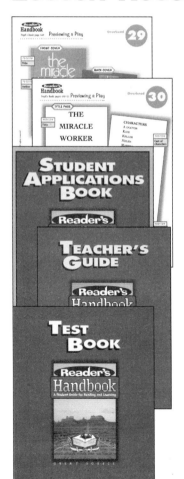

Overheads
For this lesson, use:
Overheads 29 and 30: Previewing a Play

See *Student Applications Book 10* pages 165–174.

See *Teacher's Guide* pages 296–304.

See *Test Book* for multiple-choice and short-answer tests.

See Website www.greatsource.com/rehand

WEEK 25
Lesson 1 — Organization of Lines

For use with *Reader's Handbook* pages 415–417

Goals

In this lesson, students get an overview of the concepts of poetic sound and structure and learn about the structure of poems.

Teaching Focus

Background

Earlier students got their initial exposure to the concepts of sound and structure in poetry. They learned the importance of considering punctuation, typography, layout, meter, and rhyme when reading a poem. This week, students delve deeper into the subject of sound and structure and will be able to recognize rhyme patterns and sound devices such as alliteration. They also will learn about the rhythm and meter of poems. A deeper understanding of sound and structure will enhance students' understanding and enjoyment of poems.

Instruction

Begin this lesson with an overview of the concepts of sound and structure. Students should remember that the structure of a poem shapes the poem's appearance on the page, and sound devices determine how a poem sounds when it's recited. Discuss the four elements of sound and structure in poetry: organization of lines, repeated sounds, rhymes, and rhythm or meter.

Teaching Approach

Use of the Handbook

Have students read pages 415–416 in the *Reader's Handbook*. After they've previewed Siegfried Sassoon's poem "Suicide in the Trenches," discuss what they noticed about the grouping of lines and the sound. Ask students, How are the lines laid out? What type of punctuation and capitalization does the poet use? Then have students brainstorm why it is important to notice such seemingly mundane details about a poem. Lead them to understand that each stanza can reflect a separate thought or signal the beginning of a new subject. Have students read the notes about stanza divisions on page 417. Discuss what the reader noticed about each stanza.

Extend the Handbook

Have students choose a poem to work with throughout this unit. After previewing the poem, ask them to record notes in the journal about the poem's structure.

Assessment
Ask students:

■ What elements should you notice when analyzing the structure of a poem?

■ Why is it important to analyze the organization of lines in a poem?

WEEK 25
Lesson 2   Repetition

For use with *Reader's Handbook* pages 416, 418–419

Goals

In this lesson, students explore the poetic device of repeated sounds.

Teaching Focus

Background

Remember delighting in hearing "Peter Piper picked a peck of pickled peppers" as a child? This tongue-twisting nursery rhyme is a classic example of alliteration. It is also a perfect example of what the poetic devices of alliteration and assonance accomplish in a poem. Repeated sounds add a musical dimension to poems and enhance the experience of reciting and listening to poetry. Repetition also helps to unify ideas in a poem, producing a single effect. By training students to notice repeated sounds, this lesson further enhances students' understanding and appreciation of poetry.

Instruction

Write the terms *alliteration* and *assonance* on the board and ask volunteers to define them. Many students should be aware that alliteration is the repetition of consonant sounds at the beginning of words and that assonance is the repetition of vowel sounds in accented syllables that are close together. Ask volunteers to think of examples of alliteration and assonance. Then discuss with students why poets use repeated sounds.

Teaching Approach

Use of the Handbook

Have students do a close reading of "Suicide in the Trenches" to focus on sound. Suggest that they read the poem quietly if it will help them notice repeated sounds more clearly. Have them write down or circle examples of alliteration and assonance. Then have them turn to page 418 and compare what they noticed with the notes one student made about repeated sounds. Have a volunteer recite the poem to the class. Ask students, What effect do alliteration and assonance have on the sound of the poem? Why do you think the poet chose to use these sound devices in his poem? Recommend that students use the technique of circling repeated sounds.

Extend the Handbook

Ask students to conduct a close reading of the poem they previewed during the last lesson. Ask them to notice any repeated sounds and record their thoughts in a journal entry.

Assessment

Ask students:

■ What is alliteration? What is assonance?

■ How does repetition contribute to the overall effect of a poem?

WEEK 25
Lesson 3
Sound Devices

For use with *Reader's Handbook* pages 416, 419

Goals

In this lesson, students explore the significance of sound devices.

Teaching Focus

Background

For most readers, rhyme is practically synonymous with poetry. Rhyme is the most recognizable element of verse. But few readers pause to reflect on why poets use rhyme and other sound devices. In this lesson, students learn how to mark the rhyme scheme and reflect on what effect rhyme schemes have on poems.

Instruction

Rhyme is a concept with which most students should be familiar. Explain that rhyme occurs when the ending sound of each line of a poem sounds like the ending sound of another line. Rhyme scheme refers to the pattern of rhymes in a poem. After defining these terms, ask students to brainstorm why some poems rhyme and some don't. Explain that the role of rhyme can vary from poem to poem, but rhyme can serve several purposes. It can help point to the meaning of a poem by emphasizing key words. Rhyme also can reflect a poem's mood and impart a melodic quality to it.

Teaching Approach

Use of the Handbook

Ask students to read page 419. Discuss the process of marking the rhyme scheme of a poem. Ask students, Why is it helpful to mark a poem's rhyme scheme? Then have students mark the rhyme scheme of the second and third stanzas of "Suicide in the Trenches." After they finish marking the poem, have a volunteer read the poem aloud. Ask them, What effect does the rhyme create? To help them think about why poets use rhyme, have students write a journal entry on the use of rhyme in "Suicide in the Trenches" and how rhyme affects the meaning and mood.

Extend the Handbook

Ask students to mark the rhyme scheme of the poem they've been working with throughout this unit. Then have them write a journal entry about how the rhyme scheme enhances their understanding of the meaning and mood of the poem. If the poem lacks rhyme, ask them to reflect on why the poet chose to forgo it.

Assessment

Ask students:

■ What are rhyme and rhyme scheme?

■ What is the purpose of marking a poem's rhyme scheme?

■ Why is rhyme important?

WEEK 25
Lesson 4 Meter

For use with *Reader's Handbook* pages 416, 420–422

Goals

Here students will explore the importance of meter and apply the After Reading steps of the reading process to studying the sound and structure of poems.

Teaching Focus

Background

Meter is the flow of sound produced by the words of a poem. In this lesson, students learn about meter and practice distinguishing between stressed and unstressed syllables. They also will learn how meter can affect the meaning and mood. Conclude this lesson by showing how the After Reading stage can help students grasp the significance of a poem's sound and structure.

Instruction

Write the word *meter* on the board and ask students to define it. Explain that meter, also known as *rhythm*, is the pattern of stressed and unstressed syllables in a poem. Liken meter to the beat of music. Read the first stanza of "Suicide in the Trenches" aloud, exaggerating the stressed syllables. As you read, model tapping your foot on each strong beat. Explain that there are four beats to each line in this poem.

Teaching Approach

Use of the Handbook

Have students read page 420. Discuss the symbols students can use to mark stressed and unstressed syllables. Then have students find the meter of the poem they chose to study for this unit by reading it to themselves and marking stressed and unstressed syllables on the page. Ask students to write a journal entry that reflects any changes in the poem's rhythm. Can they deduce anything about the poem's meaning from its rhythm? Suggest that they model their journal entry after the one on page 420.

Extend the Handbook

Ask students to read the After Reading steps on pages 421–422. Discuss how examining the sound and structure of a poem can deepen readers' connection to it. Underscore the usefulness of writing a poem of one's own that mimics the sound and structure of another poem. Then ask students to pause and reflect on either "Suicide in their Trenches" or the poem they selected earlier. Ask how the sound and structure of the poem helped them make a personal connection to it.

Assessment

Ask students:

■ What is meter?

■ How can the meter of a poem enhance your understanding of a poem's meaning?

WEEK 26
Lesson 1 — Before Reading a Play

For use with *Reader's Handbook* pages 446–453

Goals

In this lesson, students use Before Reading steps to prepare for reading a play.

Teaching Focus

Background

Plays have the strongest effect when they're performed. But directors and actors have to read the dialogue of a play and study its stage directions before they can rehearse a play, let alone perform it. Likewise, students will encounter plays in the classroom, and they too must have the reading tools necessary to understand the action, characters, and themes in the work. In this unit, students will review basic dramatic terminology and discover how the reading process can help them understand and connect to plays.

Instruction

Most of your students probably have read, acted in, or attended a play. Have volunteers share their experiences and discuss plays with which they are familiar. Ask students to describe what plays are and how they are structured. Point out that plays are divided into acts and scenes, which usually signal changes in the time or place of the action, or both. Next, call students' attention to the purpose of stage directions. Explain that, like other forms of fiction, plays include plot, setting, characters, and theme. Then explain how the reading process works with this genre.

Teaching Approach

Use of the Handbook

Have a volunteer start the unit by reading aloud the Introduction to Reading Drama on page 446 of the *Reader's Handbook*. Ask students to think about how the three steps of the Before Reading stage of the reading process would work with a play. After hearing their ideas, have students read pages 447–448 and 452. Emphasize the importance of summarizing. Then familiarize students with William Gibson's play *The Miracle Worker* and its subjects, Helen Keller and Annie Sullivan. Have them preview the front and back covers (page 449), the title page (page 450), and the characters (page 451). Ask volunteers to explain what they could glean about the play.

Extend the Handbook

Have students create a chart for summary notes like the one on page 453. As a class, discuss how the three tools for summarizing—Summary Notes, Magnet Summaries, and Character Maps—can help them read a play.

Assessment

Ask students:

■ How are plays like or unlike other works of fiction?

■ What are the Before Reading steps of the reading process for drama?

WEEK 26
Lesson 2   Reading with a Purpose

For use with *Reader's Handbook* pages 453–462, 464–465

Goals

In this lesson, students refine their understanding of reading actively and learn three reading tools that can help them get more from their reading of a play.

Teaching Focus

Background

Plays are different from most works of fiction. While novels tell a story through dialogue and narrative, plays contain only dialogue and stage directions. The action of the play is revealed through the dialogue and stage directions. The lack of a narrative can make it difficult for unseasoned readers to understand plays. You can help students follow the action of play more easily by teaching them the strategy of summarizing.

Instruction

Remind students about the importance of reading with a purpose. Suggest that students read with their purpose in mind and jot down their thoughts on sticky notes. Explain that they also can keep track of what's happening and answer their questions about a play by using three types of reading tools: Summary Notes, a Magnet Summary, and a Character Map. Explain the purpose of each tool and walk through the explanations on pages 456, 457, and 459.

Teaching Approach

Use of the Handbook

Ask students to recall what they learned after previewing *The Miracle Worker* during the last lesson. After having them review the questions on page 453, have them read silently the excerpt on pages 454–455. Divide students into small groups and have them discuss the excerpt and the notes they made. Then have each group practice the strategy of summarizing by completing one organizer. Discuss how the reading tools helped them to keep track of the action and characters.

Extend the Handbook

Have a volunteer read aloud the information under Connect on pages 464–465. Impress upon students that their reactions to plays are important. Connecting to characters or the play as a whole can enhance their understanding of the plot. Ask students to write a journal entry about how they connected to the excerpt.

Assessment

Ask students:

■ Why is it important to read plays with a purpose?

■ What reading tools can help you better understand plays?

WEEK 26
Lesson 3   After Reading a Play

For use with *Reader's Handbook* pages 465–468

Goals

In this lesson, students review the After Reading stage of the reading process and learn how it works with drama.

Teaching Focus

Background

Think back to the last time you saw a good play. At the end, as the actors took their bows, you stood clapping. Then you left the theater in awe, trying to digest what you'd just witnessed. Readers will experience similar feelings when they finish reading a really good play. In this lesson, you'll show students how to maximize the After Reading stage of the reading process with plays.

Instruction

Ask volunteers how they think the After Reading stage of the reading process applies to plays. Remind them that connecting to a play helps them absorb what they've read. In addition, they should Pause and Reflect and use the Reread strategy of visualizing and thinking aloud. Emphasize that rereading key scenes can help them clarify a character's actions and motivations. Explain that reviewing the notes and organizer they made while reading also can refine their understanding and help them make connections that weren't obvious during the first reading.

Teaching Approach

Use of the Handbook

Have students read page 466 and respond to the questions listed under Looking Back. Note students' responses on the board. Then divide students into groups. Ask them to imagine that they are directors who are launching a production of *The Miracle Worker* at the local playhouse. Encourage them to use the strategy of visualizing and thinking aloud to help them plan. Ask students, Who would you cast to play each role? What stage props would you need? What kind of costumes would you use? Then ask them to draw a Storyboard for the excerpt of *The Miracle Worker* that they read.

Extend the Handbook

Students can remember plays easier if they work with the script or see a filmmaker's interpretation of the action. Have students remain in their small groups and act out a key scene from *The Miracle Worker*. Then have them write a journal entry about how they benefited from doing an oral reading of the play.

Assessment

Ask students:

■ How can visualizing and thinking help you understand a play?

■ Why is doing a dramatic reading a good strategy for remembering plays?

172

WEEK 26
Lesson 4
Elements of Drama

For use with *Reader's Handbook* pages 446–468, 499–509

Goals

In this lesson, students learn more about acts, scenes, and other structural features of plays.

Teaching Focus

Background

Playwrights use plays to mirror the emotions, desires, conflicts, and reconciliations that we all have experienced by focusing intensely on a few key moments in characters' lives. They are able to capture experiences so effectively because of the tightly organized structure of plays. In this lesson, students review the structural elements of plays, such as acts, scenes, and stage directions, and learn how these help playwrights advance their plots.

Instruction

Begin by reminding students that a change in an act or scene typically reflects a change in the time or place—or both—of the action. Explain that most plays have between one and five acts. Then ask volunteers to describe what purpose acts and scenes serve in a play. Lead them to understand that acts and scenes are the building blocks that advance the plot. Then review the five main parts of a play: exposition, rising action, climax, falling action, and resolution.

Teaching Approach

Use of the Handbook

Walk students through pages 463–464. Make sure that students understand the structure of plays. It might help to have them turn to page 508 of the Elements of Drama unit in the handbook. This page provides definitions for the five main parts of the plot. Then divide students into groups and have them create a glossary of dramatic terminology. Suggest that they read the entire chapter and list the terms covered. Then they can define each term. Refer them to the Elements of Drama section on pages 499–509 if they need more information. After they complete their glossaries, discuss the terms as a class.

Extend the Handbook

Have students think of an idea for a play. Then ask them to create a Plot Diagram that identifies some of the key moments of their play. Emphasize that this is only an exercise to reinforce what they learned about the structure of plays. Their ideas don't have to be perfectly formulated.

Assessment

Ask students:

■ What is the purpose of acts and scenes in a play?

■ How is the structure of a play similar to that of a novel? How is it different?

WEEK 27
Focus on Shakespeare

For use with *Reader's Handbook* pages 485–498

Daily Lessons	Summary
Lesson 1 **A Plan for Reading Shakespeare**	Introduce a two-step plan students can use when reading a Shakespearean play.
Lesson 2 **Before Reading Shakespeare**	Help students apply Before Reading strategies to a Shakespearean play.
Lesson 3 **Reading for Sense**	Explain Step 1 of the plan: Read for sense. Explore with students idiosyncrasies of Shakespeare's language and style.
Lesson 4 **Reading for Specifics**	Explain Step 2: Read for specifics. Discuss Shakespeare's topics and voice.

Lesson Resources

See *Student Applications Book 10* pages 180–181.

See *Teacher's Guide* pages 315–319.

See *Test Book* for multiple-choice and short answer tests.

See Website www.greatsource.com/rehand

Reading a Website

For use with *Reader's Handbook* pages 513–527

Daily Lessons	Summary
Lesson 1 **Setting a Purpose**	Discuss the necessity of setting a purpose before logging on to a website.
Lesson 2 **Using a Website Profiler**	Introduce the Website Profiler to students. Explain its uses and have students apply what they've learned.
Lesson 3 **Reading with a Purpose**	Review the Read with a Purpose step of the reading process. Invite students to carefully examine the Vermeer website.
Lesson 4 **Evaluating Internet Sources**	Teach students the all-important process of evaluating a website.

Lesson Resources

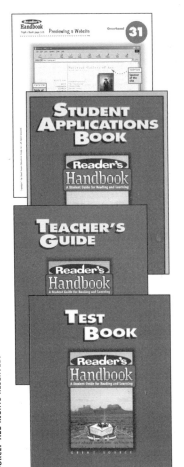

Overheads

For this lesson, use:
Overhead 31: Previewing a Website

See *Student Applications Book 10* pages 182–189.

See *Teacher's Guide* pages 331–339.

See *Test Book* for multiple-choice and short answer tests.

See Website www.greatsource.com/rehand

WEEK 27
Lesson 1

A Plan for Reading Shakespeare

For use with *Reader's Handbook* pages 485–498

Goals

This lesson offers a two-step plan for reading a play by William Shakespeare.

Teaching Focus

Background

William Shakespeare is perhaps the world's most widely read playwright. His plays explore topics and themes that are timeless. To be considered well read, high school and college students must have read—at the very least—the three or four of the most popular of Shakespeare's 38 plays. In this unit, students will learn strategies that will help them understand and enjoy Shakespearean plays.

Instruction

Begin the class by sharing your own experience with Shakespearean plays. This will help students see that everyone finds the language of his plays a bit challenging at first. Then ask students to relate their own experiences. Ask students, How is reading a Shakespearean play different from reading more contemporary plays? Explain that here they will learn a helpful plan for appreciating the language, style, topics, and voice of these unique plays.

Teaching Approach

Use of the Handbook

Have a volunteer read page 485 and the top of page 486 in the *Reader's Handbook*. Stress the importance of doing *two* careful readings of every Shakespearean play. Then ask students what it means to read for sense. Lead them to understand that, on their first reading of a Shakespearean play, it's important to get a general sense of the setting, characters, and plot. They should use the footnotes to help them, but they should avoid getting bogged down. On this first reading, they should mark those lines and scenes that appear significant to the action or themes of the play.

Extend the Handbook

Have students preview the rest of this unit. Encourage them to take notes and familiarize themselves with the components of the two-step reading plan. As a class, discuss what students hope to get out of the unit.

Assessment

Ask students:

■ How are Shakespearean plays different from contemporary plays? How are they similar?

■ What makes Shakespearean plays challenging to read?

WEEK 27
Lesson 2

Before Reading Shakespeare

For use with *Reader's Handbook* pages 486–488

Goals

In this lesson, students learn how to adapt the Before Reading steps of the reading process to Shakespeare's *Romeo and Juliet*.

Teaching Focus

Background

The Before Reading steps of the reading process are especially important with Shakespearean plays. Previewing Shakespearean plays provides students with a sort of road map to use during their careful readings. During their preview, students will encounter valuable information in the character list and play summaries that will shed light on the plot. They also will have the opportunity to peruse definitions found in the notes.

Instruction

Begin by asking volunteers to discuss how they think the Before Reading steps work with Shakespeare's plays. Then walk through the Preview Checklist on page 486 of the handbook. Point out the cast of characters in Shakespearean plays is sometimes referred to by the Latin phrase *dramatis personae*. Describe how each item on the checklist can help them prepare for careful readings.

Teaching Approach

Use of the Handbook

Offer background on *Romeo and Juliet* as needed. Then have students do their own previews of the title page (page 487) and part of the prologue (page 488). Ask them to write preview notes using the Preview Checklist as a guide. Then have volunteers discuss what they learned from previewing each item on the checklist. Have a volunteer summarize the plot. Remind students of the value of summarizing.

Extend the Handbook

Ask students to get a paperback copy or download from the Internet the full text of *Romeo and Juliet*. Have them get together in small groups and preview the entire first act.

Assessment

Ask students:

■ What items should you pay attention to when you preview a Shakespearean play?

■ How is previewing a Shakespearean play similar to previewing a contemporary play? How is it different?

WEEK 27
Lesson 3   Reading for Sense

For use with *Reader's Handbook* pages 489–493

Goals

In this lesson, students learn about Shakespeare's language and style.

Teaching Focus

Background

Many students can quote such famous lines as "To be or not to be; that is the question," even if they don't necessarily know that these lines come from Shakespearean plays. Students sometimes think that the unfamiliar words and Elizabethan style preclude them from understanding the plays themselves. In this lesson, students will learn useful strategies for understanding Shakespeare's language and style.

Instruction

Remind students that the purpose of the first reading is to get a sense of what happens and what the characters are like. Familiarize them with methods for deciphering the language in Shakespearean plays, such as reading footnotes and using a Double-entry Journal. To keep track of what they read, they can use the reading tool of Summary Notes. Then discuss Shakespeare's style with students, and define the terms *blank verse* and *rhyming couplet*. Point out the tips for understanding Shakespeare's style: reading dialogue aloud and rewriting inverted lines to make them easier to follow. Choose a passage from *Romeo and Juliet* as a way of modeling this process for students.

Teaching Approach

Use of the Handbook

Walk through pages 489–493 with students. Have them pay special attention to the word list on page 491. Then divide students into groups and have them select a passage from Act I of *Romeo and Juliet* to read for sense. Ask them to point out any patterns that emerge in the language and style of the play. They also should use a graphic organizer similar to the one on page 492 to summarize what's happening in the passage. Reconvene as a class and have students discuss what they found.

Extend the Handbook

Have students remain in groups and continue their reading of *Romeo and Juliet*. Remind them to have group members read passages aloud to help them comprehend the language and style better. Have them create Summary Notes for each new scene.

Assessment

Ask students:

■ What makes Shakespeare's language and style different from other playwrights?

■ How can reading lines and passages aloud help you understand the language and style?

WEEK 27
Lesson 4

Reading for Specifics

For use with *Reader's Handbook* pages 493–498

Goals

This lesson teaches students how to read for specifics and familiarizes them with Shakespeare's voice and common themes.

Teaching Focus

Background

Romeo and Juliet explores two of Shakespeare's favorite themes: love and revenge. Part of the appeal of his plays is that Shakespeare delved into both beautiful and troubling aspects of human nature in verse that was unfalteringly melodious. In this lesson, students learn to read with an eye toward common topics in Shakespeare's plays and his unique voice.

Instruction

Refresh students' memories about the two-step plan for reading Shakespeare. Remind them that during the second reading, they should examine characters, plot developments, and themes more closely. Refer to page 494 and show them three types of graphic organizers that they can use to make the most of the second reading—Setting Charts, Plot Diagrams, and Character Development Charts. Then discuss the Shakespearean themes of love and revenge, and familiarize students with the graphic organizers they can use to identify themes. Finally, discuss Shakespeare's unique voice and show how Paraphrase Charts can help them make a personal connection to their favorite lines in Shakespeare's plays.

Teaching Approach

Use of the Handbook

Have students return to their small groups and reread *Romeo and Juliet*. Ask them to work together to clarify points about the characters and plot and create different organizers. Then have them look at the Web and Cause-Effect Organizer on pages 495–496. Suggest that they broaden the Web with other significant words and lines. Then have each member of the group create Paraphrase Charts for their favorite lines from *Romeo and Juliet*.

Extend the Handbook

Have students remain in their small groups. Ask them to finish reading and discuss the theme in *Romeo and Juliet*. Finish by asking students to write a journal entry about their experience using the two-step plan. Did they find it helpful?

Assessment

Ask students:

■ How can reading for specifics enhance understanding of Shakespearean plays?

■ What reading tools are helpful for reading Shakespeare's plays?

WEEK 28
Lesson 1

Setting a Purpose

For use with *Reader's Handbook* pages 513–519, 523

Goals

In this lesson, students learn to use the strategy of asking pointed questions in order to set a clear purpose for reading a website.

Teaching Focus

Background

So widespread has surfing the Internet become that students have probably used it to order movie tickets, download their favorite music, or research interesting topics. What they may not have done, however, is refined a thorough approach to using the Web. In this unit, you'll show students why it's important to set a purpose before logging on to the Internet.

Instruction

Begin by asking students whether they have specific techniques for reading a website. Then ask students how they think the Before Reading stage of the reading process works with websites. Talk about the importance of setting a purpose. Explain that once students have determined their topic, they should ask themselves some general questions such as the ones on page 514. Then they should ask more specific questions about the type of information they seek. Emphasize the importance of taking notes during this process.

Teaching Approach

Use of the Handbook

Divide students into groups and have them research Vermeer's life and work as though they were writing a paper about him. Ask them to set a purpose by answering the general questions on page 514 of the handbook and then write more specific questions about what they need to find. Then, reconvene as a class and compare their questions with the ones under Set a Purpose on page 514. Walk students through pages 515–519 and page 523 of the handbook too. Point out that previewing a website is similar to previewing a textbook.

Extend the Handbook

Have students preview another website about Vermeer. Ask them to assess whether the website will help them achieve their purpose for reading. Encourage them to note what they found on the website. Then ask each group to discuss the website with the class.

Assessment

Ask students:

■ In what ways is a website similar to a textbook? In what ways is it different?

■ How does the Before Reading stage of the reading process apply to websites?

WEEK 28
Lesson 2 — Using a Website Profiler

For use with *Reader's Handbook* pages 520, 524

Goals

In this lesson, students learn the importance of reading websites critically.

Teaching Focus

Background

Websites are arguably the most democratic means for publishing information. Anyone with access to a computer can create a website and disseminate any type of knowledge without being censored or regulated. The very thing that makes websites beneficial to society, however, also makes them dangerous. Because website creators are not required to edit or fact-check their content, readers have to constantly question the veracity of what they read on the Internet. The strategy of reading critically and taking notes in Website Profilers can help students evaluate the credibility of websites and catalog their search results.

Instruction

Ask students to discuss who creates websites, and lead them to see that any individual, corporation, or organization can produce one. Point out the importance of interrogating and even double-checking the information they find on the Internet. Then discuss with students the purposes for creating a Website Profiler. Emphasize that they can use this reading tool to analyze the reliability of a site. By creating a Profiler, students also make a permanent record of each website they visit in case they need to retrace their steps or note the source of information in a bibliography. Talk to students about the different headings in a Website Profiler and how to use them.

Teaching Approach

Use of the Handbook

Have a volunteer read aloud the section on reading critically at the top of page 520. Then walk students through the six steps for reading a website critically and discuss the Website Profiler. Have students read page 524 on their own. As a class, discuss how reading critically and using a Website Profiler can help students connect to what they've read.

Extend the Handbook

Have students visit another website they know. Encourage them to follow the six steps for reading a website critically. Ask them to complete a Website Profiler to evaluate the usefulness and reliability of it.

Assessment

Ask students:

■ Why do you need to read websites critically?

■ How can a Website Profiler help you evaluate a website?

Reading with a Purpose

For use with *Reader's Handbook* pages 521–524

Goals

In this lesson, students learn reading and note-taking strategies that keep them focused while they read a website.

Teaching Focus

Background
With so many enticing links and multimedia features, websites can make students lose sight of their purpose for reading. Students also can literally become lost while reading a website if they don't understand how websites are organized. In this lesson, they will learn strategies for staying focused and getting the most out of websites.

Instruction
Website designers, like book writers, use categories to organize information, but those categories don't follow a chronological sequence as books do. Explain that links can help students access exactly what they need, but they also can distract students from their purpose. Suggest that students read with a purpose by keeping their research questions in mind as they read. Then they can take notes or print out information. A Web can help organize the answers to their questions. Impress upon students the importance of giving credit to websites. If they copy and paste information without using quotation marks or footnotes, they will be committing plagiarism.

Teaching Approach

Use of the Handbook
Ask students to read pages 521–523 to reinforce what you've told them. Then ask them to log on to the National Gallery website and read the information on Vermeer. Remind them to use their list of specific questions to organize their reading and keep them on task. They also should create a Web and enter notes into it. Suggest that they continue to read critically and complete a Website Profiler after they have finished taking notes about Vermeer. Refer them to page 524 and ask, How would you assess the Gallery's point of view and expertise? What connection did you make to the content of the pages you perused?

Extend the Handbook
Have students use the process of reading with a purpose to approach the website that they consulted during Lessons 1 and 2. Ask them to follow their reading plan again and record their findings using a Web. Remind them to create a Website Profiler to analyze the usefulness of the site and detail their reaction to it.

Assessment
Ask students:

■ How can you avoid plagiarism when researching on the web?

■ In what ways will you change your approach to websites as a result of this lesson?

182

WEEK 28
Lesson 4
Evaluating Internet Sources

For use with *Reader's Handbook* pages 525–527

Goals

This lesson teaches students how to use the reading strategy of skimming to assess the reliability of websites.

Teaching Focus

Background

A wealth of information can be found on the World Wide Web, but much of it is of dubious quality. Some sites only serve commercial purposes while others reflect the biases of their creators. Often, websites sponsored by government agencies, organizations, and educational institutions offer more reliable information than retail websites. To take advantage of the best the Web has to offer, students need a surefire strategy for identifying the most authoritative websites. In this lesson, students learn how to discern which websites will meet their needs.

Instruction

Ask students to describe how they determine the reliability of a website. List their ideas on the board. Emphasize that it's crucial for students to question what they read on websites and apply exacting standards to them. Explain that the rereading strategy of skimming is a useful way to evaluate whether a website is trustworthy.

Teaching Approach

Use of the Handbook

Have students read page 525. Then walk them through the tips for skimming a website on page 526. The elements in the left column can help them identify whether the site will meet their needs, while the elements on the right provide clues about what to avoid. Caution students to avoid sites that are poorly organized and littered with advertisements and irrelevant graphics. Compare these lists with the list that students generated. Then have students read pages 526–527, which offer tips for remembering and making connections to what they read on websites.

Extend the Handbook

Have students use the tips for skimming a website and evaluate a site. Have students write a journal entry that evaluates the site's reliability. Ask students, What factors lead you to rate the site one way or another? As a class, discuss how their strategies for reading websites will change as a result of this lesson.

Assessment

Ask students:

■ What are useful tips for skimming a website?

■ How can the strategies of reading critically and skimming help you evaluate a website?

WEEK 29
Reading a Graphic

For use with *Reader's Handbook* pages 540–553

Daily Lessons	Summary
Lesson 1 **Before Reading a Graphic**	Explore with students various types of graphics. Discuss how the steps of the Before Reading stage can help them understand information in a graphic.
Lesson 2 **Using the Strategy: Paraphrasing**	Activate students' prior knowledge of paraphrasing. Explain the benefits of using the strategy with graphics.
Lesson 3 **How Graphics Are Organized**	Work with students as they familiarize themselves with the basic organizational elements of graphics.
Lesson 4 **Drawing Conclusions from Graphics**	Build an understanding of After Reading strategies students can use to analyze the information in graphics sources.

Lesson Resources

Overheads
For this lesson, use:
Overhead 32: Previewing a Graphic
Overhead 33: How to Read a Graphic

See *Student Applications Book 10* pages 190–197.

See *Teacher's Guide* pages 346–354.

See *Test Book* for multiple-choice and short answer tests.

See Website www.greatsource.com/rehand

Reading a Driver's Handbook

For use with *Reader's Handbook* pages 571–580

Daily Lessons	Summary
Lesson 1 **Before Reading a Driver's Handbook**	Work with students as they apply the Before Reading steps of the reading process to a driver's education handbook.
Lesson 2 **Using the Strategy: Skimming**	Work with students as they use the strategy of skimming to get a general sense of the content and sort important from unimportant details in a driver's handbook.
Lesson 3 **How a Driver's Handbook Is Organized**	Explore the organization of a driver's handbook. Discuss the importance of chapter heads and subheads.
Lesson 4 **Preparing for the Written Examination**	Review strategies students can use to prepare for your state's written examination.

Lesson Resources

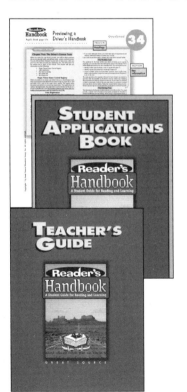

Overheads

For this lesson, use:

Overhead 34: Previewing a Driver's Handbook

See *Student Applications Book 10* pages 198–204.

See *Teacher's Guide* pages 365–371.

See *Test Book* for multiple-choice and short answer tests.

See Website www.greatsource.com/rehand

WEEK 29
Lesson 1
Before Reading a Graphic

For use with *Reader's Handbook* pages 540–544

Goals

In this lesson, students will explore various types of graphics and how to use the Before Reading stage of the reading process to understand information presented in graphic form.

Teaching Focus

Background
The Introduction to Reading Graphics in the *Reader's Handbook* (page 540) explores various reasons that students need to learn how to read a graphic. Explain that you will provide students with specific techniques they can use to understand and evaluate the graphics they come across when reading.

Instruction
Direct students to their history, math, or science textbooks. Have them thumb through their books, keeping a tally of the number and types of graphics they find. Ask students why the number of graphics used in reading material has increased over the years. Then ask a student to review for the class the three steps of the Before Reading stage of the reading process. Finish by asking students to preview the sample graphics shown in the handbook.

Teaching Approach

Use of the Handbook
Read aloud page 540 and the Goals box on page 541. Then have them turn to the Elements of Graphics section of the handbook (pages 554–567). Explain that they will want to refer to this section as they make their way through the unit. Then have students return to page 541 and begin reading. Ask one student to reread pages 30–32 (The Reading Process) and then summarize the purpose of each step of the Before Reading stage. Have students preview and make notes on "Digital Kids" (page 543). Finish by having students read page 544.

Extend the Handbook
Divide the class into four groups. Assign one of the following types of graphics to each group: chart or table, pie graph, line graph, and diagram. Have the groups find 3–5 other examples of their type of graphic by looking in newspapers, magazines, and textbooks.

Assessment
Ask students:

■ What are the most common types of graphics you have to read?

■ How can the Before Reading steps of the reading process help you read graphics?

WEEK 29
Lesson 2

Using the Strategy: Paraphrasing

For use with *Reader's Handbook* pages 544–545

Goals

Here students use the strategy of paraphrasing to enhance their understanding of the information presented in a graphic.

Teaching Focus

Background

Page 544 of the *Reader's Handbook* contains a five-step plan students can follow when reading a graphic. Key to the success of this plan is the strategy of paraphrasing. Paraphrasing, or retelling, means extracting key information from a graphic and putting it into your own words. Like all of the strategies discussed in the handbook, paraphrasing requires students to be active, rather than passive, readers of a text.

Instruction

Ask students to name the steps they normally follow when reading a graphic, and write each step on the board. Next to the list students generate, write the steps presented on page 544 of the handbook. Point out similarities and differences between the two lists. Then reintroduce the strategy of paraphrasing. Activate students' prior knowledge of the strategy and then explore how they might use the strategy with a graphic. Lead them to see that paraphrasing can help them understand and remember key information.

Teaching Approach

Use of the Handbook

Direct students' attention to the Plan for Reading a Graphic on page 544. Read the steps aloud and compare them to the process students normally follow. Then direct students to read page 545 together. Ask group members to use the strategy to help them process key facts and details from "Digital Kids."

Extend the Handbook

Ask groups to return to the graphics they found in the previous lesson. Have groups brainstorm characteristics of the graphic and then work together to write a summary of it in which they discuss the "big picture."

Assessment

Ask students:

■ What are the five steps in the Plan for Reading a Graphic?

■ What is paraphrasing, and how can it help you get more from reading a graphic?

How Graphics Are Organized

For use with *Reader's Handbook* pages 547–549

Goals

In this lesson, students examine key organizational elements in a graphic.

Teaching Focus

Background

Understanding organization is a key component of reading a graphic. Here you'll provide an overview of the structure of most graphics and then offer students the opportunity to apply what they've learned. In addition, you'll work with the class to develop a shared vocabulary that they can use when discussing various elements of graphics. Refer students to Elements of Graphics (pages 554–567) as needed.

Instruction

Explain to students that, even though graphics come in many forms, they all share certain organizational features. Then ask students to return to the graphics they examined in their history, science, or math textbooks. Point out such common features as titles, units, legends, scales, and axes. Ask students, How can learning about these features make it easier for you to read a graphic? Have students apply what they've learned to the graphic "Digital Kids."

Teaching Approach

Use of the Handbook

Have students turn to page 547. Point out the title, legend, and axes in "Digital Kids." Explain that, in all graphics, text and picture are equally important. Remind students that taking notes as they read can help them become more actively involved in the text. Finish the lesson with a brief discussion of Read with a Purpose and making personal connections to the information in a graphic.

Extend the Handbook

After groups identify the "big picture" presented in their graphic, have them paraphrase its key facts and details. Suggest they use a Paraphrase Chart like the one found on page 546.

If students need additional practice in reading a graphic, have them complete pages 190–197 in *Student Applications Book 10*.

Assessment

Ask students:

■ Why is it important to examine elements of graphics such as legends, units, and scales?

■ How does understanding the organization of a graphic help you interpret the information?

WEEK 29
Lesson 4

Drawing Conclusions from Graphics

For use with *Reader's Handbook* pages 550–553

Goals

Here students learn how to read critically and draw conclusions to get the most out of graphic sources.

Teaching Focus

Background

Once students are able to paraphrase information in a graphic, their next step is to draw conclusions about what that information means. An important aspect of drawing conclusions is evaluating the reliability of the information and the source. In this lesson, students will learn to reflect upon and think critically about the facts from a graphic source.

Instruction

Ask students to think about the process involved in drawing conclusions. Point out that readers use the same process, or follow the same steps, when drawing conclusions about the information in a graphic. Remind the class that, like most texts, graphics are open to interpretation. Explain that in this lesson students will sharpen and refine their ability to draw conclusions and read critically. Then, they'll apply what they've learned to reading a graphic.

Teaching Approach

Use of the Handbook

Have students read the information on pages 550–551. Discuss the importance of reading critically before drawing conclusions from the data presented in the graphic. Point to the four questions in Column 1 of the Critical Reading Chart and explain that these are the kinds of questions good readers ask themselves. Read aloud the information on evaluating a graphic's sources (page 552) and finish with a discussion of the techniques students can use to remember what they've learned.

Extend the Handbook

Offer students a set of data and have them create graphics that reflect this information. Leave it to students to choose the type of graphic they create, but they should explain the choice they made. Ask students to trade graphics. Have them use the reading process to read and interpret their partner's work.

Assessment

Ask students:

■ How can you read graphics critically?

■ Why might two readers draw two different conclusions from the same graphic?

WEEK 30
Lesson 1

Before Reading a Driver's Handbook

For use with *Reader's Handbook* pages 571–575

Goals

Here students learn how to apply the Before Reading stage to a driver's handbook.

Teaching Focus

Background

Students in the tenth grade will be particularly motivated, even eager, to read your state's driver's handbook. Take advantage of their interest and review students' understanding of the Before Reading stage of the reading process.

Instruction

Begin by asking students to preview pages 571–580 of the *Reader's Handbook*. Then have volunteers explain how they'd use the Before Reading stage with this text. Lead students to see that each time they pick up a driver's handbook, their purpose might be slightly different, but for the most part it will involve finding out what they need to know to pass the written driver's exam. Be sure to discuss the importance of skimming the book's table of contents as they preview.

Teaching Approach

Use of the Handbook

Read aloud the lesson introduction on page 571. Discuss the goals listed and encourage students to make notes about their own. Then have a volunteer read the information on how to set a purpose, preview, and make a plan for reading a driver's handbook. Direct students' attention to the table of contents on page 573. Make the point that this page may be one of the most important in the book since it shows students the major topics they'll be tested on. Finish by discussing skimming and the Key Word or Topic Notes organizer on page 575.

Extend the Handbook

Download or get a copy of your state driving manual. Divide the book into five or six parts; create the same number of student groups. Assign one part to each group. Have group members set a purpose, preview, and plan for a careful reading of their part of the driver's manual. Ask a group secretary to record notes on a Preview Chart similar to the one on page 750.

Assessment

Ask students:

■ How does a driver's handbook differ from other types of nonfiction texts?

■ Why do you think the strategy of skimming is particularly useful with this type of reading?

190

Using the Strategy: Skimming

For use with *Reader's Handbook* pages 573–576

Goals

In this lesson, students use skimming with a driver's handbook.

Teaching Focus

Background

The strategy of skimming is a valuable one for several reasons. First, it can help readers find the information they need in a minimal amount of time. Second, skimming encourages students to separate important from unimportant details in a reading. This means that it is valuable to use both when *preparing for* a test and when *taking* a test.

Instruction

Ask students to read silently page 576. Discuss Reading with a Purpose and reiterate the importance of completing a Key Word or Topic Notes organizer as they read. Then have students read the sample driver's handbook chapter, which explores the requirements for a state driving exam. Ask them to take notes as they read and then compare what they wrote with the sample on page 576.

Teaching Approach

Use of the Handbook

Discuss the usefulness of an organizer such as the Key Word or Topic Notes chart. Have students read carefully on page 576 how to use the organizer. After they finish the excerpt, have students examine the Web on page 577. They may want to make an organizer similar to this when preparing for their exam. Explain that the reading process can help them before, during, and even after they take their driver's exam.

Extend the Handbook

Have students continue their work with a driver's manual. Ask them to apply the During Reading strategies to the text and then discuss what they've read as a group. Have students work together to make Key Topic or Summary Notes that explore their chapter.

Assessment

Ask students:

■ What reading strategy can help you get more from a driver's handbook?

■ Why is it important to make a connection to the material in a driver's handbook?

WEEK 30
Lesson 3

How a Driver's Handbooks Is Organized

For use with *Reader's Handbook* pages 573–574

Goals

Here students learn the standard organization for a driver's handbook and explore the importance of the book's headings and subheadings.

Teaching Focus

Background

Over the course of the year, students have been considering how the organization of a piece of writing can affect their understanding. By now, they should understand that knowing a little something about organization ahead of time can make the text easier to read, understand, and respond to. In this lesson, you'll discuss key organizational features of a driver's handbook.

Instruction

Start by asking students about their experiences with real-world writing, such as writing for work, instruction manuals, game directions, and so on. Ask students, What organizational features crop up again and again in this type of writing? What aspects of the writing are most challenging? Then direct students' attention to a more focused discussion of the organization of a driver's handbook. Discuss key features in this type of text. Point out features that students can use to their advantage when studying for the driver's exam.

Teaching Approach

Use of the Handbook

Have students study the sample driver's handbook pages to get a sense of the organization of this type of text. Point out to students that they can expect to see short paragraphs, bulleted lists, and diagrams and pictures throughout. Ask students, Why do you think a driver's handbook is so visual? How can you make the visual nature of the text work to your advantage?

Extend the Handbook

As a class, compare the organization of their state driver's manual to the one in the *Reader's Handbook*. Ask students to discuss the importance of the manual's headings and how they can use them when studying for the written examination.

Assessment

Ask students:

■ What are some of the key features of a driver's handbook?

■ How are manuals often organized?

WEEK 30
Lesson 4
Preparing for the Written Examination

For use with *Reader's Handbook* pages 578–580

Goals

In this lesson, students will learn how the After Reading steps of the reading process can be used to help them prepare for their state driving exam.

Teaching Focus

Background

Few students read a driver's handbook for pleasure. Rather, they read with a purpose in mind—to pass the written examination for the driving test. Here you'll show students how they can use the After Reading steps when studying for the exam.

Instruction

Begin by discussing the three After Reading steps (Pause and Reflect, Reread, and Remember) with students. Have volunteers explain the purpose of each step and how it might work with a driver's handbook. Ask students to focus particularly on various Remember strategies. Help them find a way to memorize and then recall the rules, signage, and restrictions that they're sure to be tested on.

Teaching Approach

Use of the Handbook

Point out that with a driver's handbook the Remember step of the reading process may be most important. After a discussion of all three steps of the After Reading stage, ask students to turn to page 578 in their handbooks. Have them read the page silently. Then ask them to answer the Looking Back questions on their own. Explain that, if they can't answer yes to both questions, they'll need to do some rereading. Next, review the rereading strategy of visualizing and thinking aloud. Students may recall from a previous unit that drawing a rule or concept can make it easier to remember. Point out that they may want to use this strategy when they take the written driver's test.

Extend the Handbook

Ask each group to return to the state driver's manual they've been using all week. Have students write and then present a summary of key instructions, terms, and rules. Then ask groups to get together one last time to write a five- to ten-question practice test that explores their part of the handbook. When all groups have finished, put the tests together into a packet and distribute to the entire class.

Assessment

Ask students:

■ Why is rereading important for a driver's manual?

■ Why is the Remember step probably the most important?

WEEK 31

Reading for Tests and Test Questions

For use with *Reader's Handbook* pages 599–616

Daily Lessons	Summary
Lesson 1 **Preparing for a Test**	Help students activate prior knowledge and build background about strategies that work with in-class and standardized tests.
Lesson 2 **A Test-taking Plan**	Discuss a three-step plan that students can use with virtually any type of test.
Lesson 3 **Answering Test Questions**	Explore how the strategy of skimming can help students find the correct answers to test questions.
Lesson 4 **After Reading a Test**	Review the purpose of visualizing and thinking aloud. Model how to use the strategy with challenging test questions.

Lesson Resources

Overheads

For this lesson, use:

Overhead 35: Previewing a Test
Overhead 36: Reading Fact or Recall Questions
Overhead 37: Reading Inference Questions
Overhead 38: Reading Essay Questions

See *Student Applications Book 10* pages 210–216.

See *Teacher's Guide* pages 382–390.

See *Test Book* for multiple-choice and short answer tests.

See Website www.greatsource.com/rehand

WEEK 32

Focus on History Tests

For use with *Reader's Handbook* pages 638–642

Daily Lessons	Summary
Lesson 1 **History Tests: An Overview**	Discuss with students elements of history tests.
Lesson 2 **Reading History Test Questions**	Explore various types of history test questions.
Lesson 3 **Answering History Test Questions**	Introduce specific strategies students can use to answer history test questions.
Lesson 4 **Answering Questions about Graphics and Primary Sources**	Help students explore techniques for answering graphics questions and questions that involve primary sources, such as documents and letters.

Lesson Resources

See *Student Applications Book 10* pages 224–226.

See *Teacher's Guide* pages 404–407.

See *Test Book* for multiple-choice and short answer tests.

See Website www.greatsource.com/rehand

Preparing for a Test

For use with *Reader's Handbook* pages 599–605

Goals

In this lesson, you'll introduce the test-taking section of the *Reader's Handbook* and discuss techniques students can use to strengthen their scores on various school, state, and national assessment tests.

Teaching Focus

Background

In high school—the tenth and eleventh grades in particular—test scores take on great importance, which means that students' test-taking anxiety will run at an all-time high. You can help alleviate this anxiety by discussing preparation techniques students can use. Use this lesson as a way of introducing the testing section of the handbook.

Instruction

Students may need to use this section of the *Reader's Handbook* at various times over the course of the year, so it's a good idea to begin by familiarizing students with what's offered. To help, have them preview the entire test-taking section of the handbook, including the Reading for Tests chapter and the six Focus sections (pages 598–655). For purposes of discussion, have students create a Magnet Summary or Web that shows what they noticed in their preview.

Teaching Approach

Use of the Handbook

Have students turn to and read carefully pages 599–600. Point out the two purpose questions and the Preview Checklist. Finish with a discussion of tests and quizzes students have taken in the past several weeks. Ask students, Which of these exams were most challenging and why? Remind students of the causal relationship between preparing thoroughly beforehand and doing well on the test. Begin exploring the test-preparation strategies discussed in the handbook.

Extend the Handbook

Download a sample standardized test from your state's testing site, or visit one of the national testing sites (such as www.ets.org) and look for sample tests that you can use with students. Give a copy of the sample test to each student and ask that they apply the Before Reading stage of the reading process to the test. Have them write their preview notes on an organizer of their choice.

Assessment

Ask students:

- What is your purpose when reading a test question?

- How should you preview a test?

WEEK 31
Lesson 2
A Test-taking Plan

For use with *Reader's Handbook* pages 603–611

Goals

Here students will explore a three-step plan they can use with virtually any type of school or standardized test.

Teaching Focus

Background

As you know, school-based exams contain multiple-choice, true-false, short-answer, and the dreaded essay questions. Test questions can be further divided into two groupings: fact-based and inferential. In this lesson, you'll introduce a three-step plan students can use with all types of questions: Step 1, Read the passage (or prompt); Step 2, Read the questions and look for key words; and Step 3, Skim the passage (or prompt) for answers or clues about answers.

Instruction

Begin with a discussion of the three-step plan shown on page 605. Explain that completing an active reading of the passage or prompt is key to answering related questions correctly. Whenever possible, students should highlight, underline, and make margin notes about important points. After students read and note the marking of the sample passage (Heinrich Böll's "The Laugher"), begin your instruction of the strategy of skimming.

Teaching Approach

Use of the Handbook

Have students skim pages 606–611 of the *Reader's Handbook*. Discuss key information about various types of questions students can expect to see on high school tests. (Use pages 603–604 to provide examples.) Then ask students to read each question on the sample test. Be sure they mark key words as they go.

Extend the Handbook

Ask students to revisit the sample standardized test you downloaded from the Internet and apply the strategies they learned here to those test questions. Then ask volunteers to comment on the ratio of factual to inferential questions on the test. Point out that students usually can expect twice as many (or more) critical thinking as they can factual questions on most standardized exams.

For additional practice, have students complete pages 210–216, 217–219, 220–221, 222–223 of *Student Applications Book 10*.

Assessment

Ask students:

■ Why is it important to note the key words in each question?

■ What is the purpose of skimming and how can it help you during an exam?

WEEK 31
Lesson 3

Answering Test Questions

For use with *Reader's Handbook* page 606–611

Goals

Here students will discuss strategies they can use to answer test questions.

Teaching Focus

Background

After students have read the passage or prompt and marked key words in the questions, they need to begin thinking about strategies they can use to figure out the correct answers. Skimming can help here because it enables students to "screen out" irrelevant details and "zoom in" on the information needed.

Instruction

Review the three steps of the test-taking plan. Explain that here you'll focus on Step 3, Skim the passage (or prompt) for answers or clues about answers. Explain to students that sometimes they'll be able to find the answer to a question in the passage itself. Explain that, in other cases, students will need to make inferences about answers. Model the process by thinking aloud answers to questions 4 and 5.

Teaching Approach

Use of the Handbook

Have students read silently pages 606–607. Review the kinds of questions listed at the bottom of page 607 and discuss particular challenges of each. Then walk through pages 608–611 with students. Focus on answering essay questions and point out the Focus on English Tests and Focus on Writing Tests lessons. Next, have students work in small groups to discuss and then answer the questions on the sample test. Finish by having them read the essay question and comment on what they need to do to write the essay.

Extend the Handbook

Ask students to answer the questions on a sample of the standardized test they are using in their state. Have individual students present a sample question to the class and think aloud about how they answered it.

For additional practice with writing essay answers, ask students to complete pages 217–219, 220–221, 222–223. of *Student Applications Book 10*.

Assessment

Ask students:

■ What is a good plan for answering test questions?

■ How can the strategy of skimming help with test questions?

WEEK 31
Lesson 4 — After Reading a Test

For use with *Reader's Handbook* pages 613–616

Goals

In this lesson, students examine After Reading strategies to use with a test and discuss the role visualizing and thinking aloud plays in answering test questions.

Teaching Focus

Background

Many students run out of time before they can finish the final part of an exam. The end of an exam might contain questions that are weighted more heavily than questions at the beginning. In this lesson, you'll discuss how to budget time effectively and offer specific solutions to time problems. These solutions include skimming for answers rather than rereading entire passages, looking at the big picture in a graphic rather than getting bogged down in the details, and eliminating incorrect answer choices whenever possible. For writing tests, students should become "expert users" of one type of organizer so that creating the organizer on the day of the test will take very little of their time.

Instruction

After your discussion of time constraints and possible solutions, walk students through the After Reading information on pages 613–616. Explain the importance of the Pause and Reflect step and how valuable self-assessment is when it comes to taking a test. Once students have determined which questions they'd like to revisit, they can use the strategy of visualizing and thinking aloud to rethink their answers.

Teaching Approach

Use of the Handbook

Divide the class into three small groups. Assign one step of the After Reading stage to each group. Have group members read the relevant pages in the handbook and then make Summary Notes that explore the most important points. Finish the lesson by modeling how to apply After Reading steps to a challenging test question.

Extend the Handbook

Have students reread the essay question on page 604 and then create a Main Idea Organizer that shows how they would answer the question. Remind students that all good essays contain a clear and succinct thesis statement as well as three or more supporting details. After students have finished their organizers, invite students who want extra credit to write the summary assigned in the prompt.

Assessment

Ask students:

■ What does it mean to visualize and think aloud during a test?

■ What tool can help you prepare to write an essay?

History Tests: An Overview

For use with *Reader's Handbook* page 638

Goals

In this lesson, students discuss the general characteristics of history tests and their experiences with this type of exam.

Teaching Focus

Background

By now, students will have had plenty of history tests. To perform successfully on a history test, students must understand what will be covered on the test and then use their textbook, class notes, websites, and so on to study the people, places, and events specified.

Instruction

Invite students to share their experiences with history tests. What makes them challenging? Work with students to make a list of history test elements. Their list should include the types of questions usually asked, how most tests are organized, and the kinds of responses that tend to receive the highest marks. At this point, focus on how students prepare for these history tests and the rate of success they've had with each approach. Students may appreciate hearing your experiences with these kinds of tests as well.

Teaching Approach

Use of the Handbook

Use the handbook to support the lesson. Have a volunteer read aloud the introduction on page 638 and the three goals listed in the box. Discuss with students techniques for preparing for a history test. Explain that students will learn a variety of test-taking tips in the next few lessons. Point out that many of the tips will work with any type of exam students take.

Extend the Handbook

Invite students to complete this sentence: *The last time I took a history test. . . .* Encourage them to offer a detailed analysis of how they prepared for the test, how the test was organized, and the questions that were easiest and most challenging for them.

Assessment

Ask students:

■ What part of a history test do you find the easiest to complete? What part is most challenging?

■ What is one strategy you use while getting ready for a history test?

WEEK 32
Lesson 2

Reading History Test Questions

For use with *Reader's Handbook* page 639

Goals

In this lesson, students will explore various types of history test questions.

Teaching Focus

Background

History tests are meant to help students demonstrate their knowledge of important historic events and the people, places, and dates associated with those events. History tests often contain at least one of the following types of questions: open response or short answer, true-false, multiple-choice, and matching. Most history tests also will require one or more essay-length response. In this lesson, you'll discuss various types of history test questions and the strategies students can use to answer them.

Instruction

Have students help you generate a list of different types of questions on a history test. Afterward, poll students to find out which they find easiest and which are most challenging. Give students time to explain the reasoning behind their choices. Then have students read the test-taking tips in the handbook. As students read, focus their attention on which tips work best for which types of questions. They may decide that some tips will benefit them when taking any type of test question.

Teaching Approach

Use of the Handbook

Ask volunteers to read aloud the tips on page 639. Discuss each tip in some detail. Invite students to discuss how these tips might help with the various types of test questions and which ones they have tried in the past.

Extend the Handbook

Pull students' attention back to Tip #1: Create a Top Ten List. Students can practice this strategy by making a top ten list of a topic they have recently studied in your class. You may choose to assign the entire class to work on the same topic or invite students to make lists for different topics. Have students share their lists with the rest of the class.

Assessment

Ask students:

■ What are the various types of questions you might encounter on a history test?

■ What are two tips you can use to answer questions on history tests?

Answering History Test Questions

For use with *Reader's Handbook* page 640

Goals

In this lesson, students discuss specific strategies they can use when answering history test questions.

Teaching Focus

Background

Good test takers have strategies that they can call upon to help them preview, read, and then answer test questions. As a first step, good test-takers preview the test to get a feel for how the questions are formatted and categorized. Next, they answer the questions with which they are familiar. With the more challenging questions, they might use graphic organizers to pull together the information they need to answer. Finally, when attacking difficult multiple-choice questions, they use such strategies as eliminating wrong answers and thinking aloud.

Instruction

Ask volunteers to share questions they recall from past history tests. Write a number of these questions on the board. Discuss strategies students might use to answer the questions. Then explain how to preview a history test and reiterate the importance of answering easy questions first. Use the handbook to support your discussion of test-taking strategies to use with the more challenging questions.

Teaching Approach

Use of the Handbook

Have students review the preparation tips on page 639. Then have them read page 640 to themselves. Ask a volunteer to model how to use the information in the handbook to answer one of the questions you've listed on the board. If you feel students would benefit, think aloud answers to several of the other questions.

Extend the Handbook

Divide students into small groups. Have each group write a five-question history test for another group to complete. When students are ready to exchange tests, remind them to use the strategies discussed in the handbook to help them answer the questions.

Assessment

Ask students:

■ How can answering easy questions first help you do well on a history test?

■ What test-taking tips and strategies can you use the next time you take a history exam?

Answering Questions about Graphics and Primary Sources

For use with *Reader's Handbook* pages 641–642

Goals

In this lesson, students explore techniques for answering graphics questions and questions that involve primary sources, such as documents and letters.

Teaching Focus

Background

Most history exams will contain several graphics and primary source documents, such as letters, speeches, and diary entries. Students will be asked to read the source and then interpret what it means. The purpose of these types of test questions is to examine students' ability to extract key details from a "real-world" historical source. In this lesson, you'll help students develop strategies that they can use with graphics and primary sources.

Instruction

Ask students what it means to "look at the big picture." Help them understand that it means paying attention to what is most important. Explain that examining the big picture is the first thing students should do when they come to a graphics or primary source document on a history text. In addition, they'll ask themselves such questions as, "What can the graphic/document tell me?" and "Which information appears to be most important?"

Teaching Approach

Use of the Handbook

Have a volunteer read the top of page 641 in the *Reader's Handbook*. Discuss Tip #7. Point out other helpful tips, such as making notes in the margin of your test booklet and reading the graphic from top to bottom. Then read aloud the sample question and the Think Aloud on page 642. Finish the lesson by asking a volunteer to read the last half of page 642. Give students a chance to reflect on what they've learned.

Extend the Handbook

Supply pairs of students with old history tests. Invite pairs to preview the test and start the questions they know will be easy to answer. Then have them use strategies described in the *Reader's Handbook*. When they've finished, carefully examine the techniques they used to answer the questions.

Assessment

Ask students:

■ Why is it important when reading a graphic or document to examine the "big picture"?

■ What makes test questions with graphics challenging?

WEEK 33

Focus on Math Tests

For use with *Reader's Handbook* pages 643–649

Daily Lessons	Summary
Lesson 1 **Preparing for a Math Test**	Discuss various methods students can use to prepare for a math test.
Lesson 2 **Reading Questions on a Math Test**	Activate students' prior knowledge about math test questions.
Lesson 3 **Solving Challenging Math Problems**	Introduce four test-taking tips students can use to solve more challenging problems on a math test.
Lesson 4 **Solving Problems Involving Graphics**	Review information on reading graphics presented in the *Reader's Handbook*. Have students use what they know to solve graphics questions on math tests.

Lesson Resources

See *Student Applications Book 10* pages 227–228.

See *Teacher's Guide* pages 408–411.

See *Test Book* for multiple-choice and short answer tests.

See Website www.greatsource.com/rehand

WEEK 34

Doing Research

For use with *Reader's Handbook* pages 691–712

Daily Lessons	Summary
Lesson 1 **Doing Research: An Overview**	Present an overview of the research process.
Lesson 2 **Locating Information**	Differentiate between primary and secondary sources and where students can find them.
Lesson 3 **Evaluating Sources**	Emphasize the importance of evaluating sources before presenting the research.
Lesson 4 **Tracking and Documenting Information**	Review and refine students' understanding of how to take notes on their research and document their sources.

Lesson Resources

See *Teacher's Guide* pages 424–431.

See Website www.greatsource.com/rehand

Preparing for a Math Test

For use with *Reader's Handbook* pages 643–644

Goals

In this lesson, students discuss the various methods they can use to prepare for a math test.

Teaching Focus

Background

If you were to poll your students, you would probably find that they consider math tests to be the most difficult tests of all. One reason for this is that most students don't have a clear understanding of how to prepare for this type of exam. Another is that they don't have in their tool belts a set of strategies that they can call upon when taking the test. In this lesson, you'll discuss math test "anxiety" and how students can overcome it.

Instruction

Begin by asking students what they already do to prepare for a math test. They may say they study with a friend and review homework assignments. Write students' preparation strategies on the board. Add to this list as students read the information in the *Reader's Handbook*.

Teaching Approach

Use of the Handbook

Read aloud the three goals on page 643 of the *Reader's Handbook*. Then have a volunteer read aloud the rest of page 643. Make notes on the board about each new strategy, and have students do the same in their reading journals. Remind students to refer to these strategies as needed over the course of the unit. End the lesson by asking students to read the top of page 644 and then preview the sample math pages.

Extend the Handbook

Have students thumb through their math texts and make a list of common characteristics. Ask them to list the characteristics in their reading journals and then write a summary of how each math chapter seems to be organized. Explain that understanding the organization of a chapter can make it easier for students to use when preparing for an exam.

Offer students additional practice by asking them to complete pages 227–228 in *Student Applications Book 10*.

Assessment

Ask students:

■ What is one strategy you currently use when preparing for a math test?

■ What is the purpose of previewing a math test before you begin solving the problems?

WEEK 33
Lesson 2

Reading a Math Test

For use with *Reader's Handbook* page 644

Goals

In this lesson, students apply the During Reading stage to a math test.

Teaching Focus

Background

Like other tests, math tests tend to have several different types of questions on a single exam: numeric expression questions, story or word problems, and problems involving pictures, diagrams, and other graphics. As a way of boosting their confidence level, help students become experts in a single type of question. Remind them of the importance of answering easier questions first and using a variety of strategies to help them cope with the more challenging. Most important of all is to teach students how to read a question carefully. Remind them that in a math question every word counts to some degree.

Instruction

Begin by reminding students that on most math tests the problems become sequentially more difficult. In general, then, they'll be saving the final test questions for last. Also, some problems only *look* challenging. This is often the case with word problems, especially those that contain an abundance of information. Explain that very often the question itself will provide valuable clues about the correct answer. This is why it's important to do a careful, active reading of each question, making notes as you go.

Teaching Approach

Use of the Handbook

Ask students to read page 644 in the *Reader's Handbook*. When they're finished, ask them to describe what they learned from this page. Direct their attention to the sample question and student notes. Explain that talking your way through a problem can help you understand its purpose and the direction you should take.

Extend the Handbook

Invite students to become teachers. Tell them you would like them to write a paragraph or design a poster that teaches middle school students what to do before and during a math test. Encourage them to reread handbook pages 643 and 644 for key details they missed the first time around.

Assessment

Ask students:

- Why is it important to preview a math test before you begin answering the questions?

- How are questions on math tests usually organized?

Solving Challenging Math Problems

WEEK 33
Lesson 3

For use with *Reader's Handbook* pages 645–648

Goals

In this lesson, students are introduced to four test-taking tips they can use to solve more challenging problems on a math test.

Teaching Focus

Background

Students need at their command a series of tips or techniques they can use to solve challenging math problems, including eliminating wrong answers, plugging in possible answers, visualizing, and trying easier numbers first. One or more of these techniques may be familiar to students, but all will benefit from a careful modeling of how to use the techniques and a detailed discussion of why and how they work.

Instruction

Discuss the types of math problems students find most challenging and the various methods they use to solve them. Invite volunteers to share their ideas. Then walk through the four techniques discussed in the handbook. Ask volunteers to model using the strategy with sample problems you've written on the board.

Teaching Approach

Use of the Handbook

Have students preview the four tips introduced in the *Reader's Handbook* on pages 645–648. Then divide the class into four groups and assign a tip to each group. Have the group reread its tip and then "teach" the tip to the class.

Extend the Handbook

Have each expert group come up with a second problem that can be solved with its tip. As a class, read each problem aloud and discuss which tip can be used with each problem. Students may be able to show that some problems can work well with more than one tip. Remind students that when they are taking a math test and none of these tips seem to be working for them, it is advisable to make an educated (as opposed to a random) guess about the correct answer.

Assessment

Ask students:

■ When is it a good idea to eliminate wrong answers?

■ What does it mean to "visualize the answer"?

■ How would you explain the tip "try easier numbers first"?

WEEK 33
Lesson 4

Solving Problems Involving Graphics

For use with *Reader's Handbook* pages 648–649

Goals

In this lesson, students review key information on how to read and interpret graphics and then apply what they know to the graphics on math tests.

Teaching Focus

Background

Most students are intimidated by math problems involving graphics. You can help by arming students with specific strategies they can use when they come across the figures, graphics, charts, and diagrams that are an important part of just about any math test.

Instruction

Find copies of an old math test or download a sample test from your state's testing website. Preview the test with students, paying particular attention to questions involving graphics. Then ask a volunteer to summarize how to read a graphic and the specific strategies that work well with graphics. Work together to solve the problems. End with a review of the four-step plan students should follow when taking a math test.

Teaching Approach

Use of the Handbook

Have students read pages 648–649 in the *Reader's Handbook*. Point out that it is very important to memorize key concepts and formulas *before* the test. Then have a volunteer list on the board four steps for solving a problem involving graphics. Talk about the purpose of each step and ask students to comment on what they think of the plan. Take time to model how to implement this plan.

Extend the Handbook

Discuss with students memorization techniques they've learned that can help them remember key math terms, rules, and formulas. Encourage students to make these techniques a part of the four-step plan introduced in the handbook.

Assessment

Ask students:

■ What can you do to prepare for a math test involving graphics?

■ What is the four-step plan for solving problems with graphics?

WEEK 34
Lesson 1

Doing Research: An Overview

For use with *Reader's Handbook* pages 691–712

Goals

In this lesson, students preview the research section of the *Reader's Handbook* and compare the reading process to the research process.

Teaching Focus

Background

The Reader's Almanac section of the handbook (pages 691–757) has three parts: a research section, the Strategy Handbook, and the Reading Tools section. In this lesson and the three that follow, students will explore the research section. Highlight the clear parallels between the research and reading processes.

Instruction

When modified slightly, the seven steps of the reading process—set a purpose, preview, plan, read with a purpose, connect, pause and reflect, reread, and remember—can become a simple research process students can use with any academic subject. On pages 692–694 you'll find a discussion of the reading and research processes together. As an opening activity, list the steps of the reading process on the board. Then ask students to think about how each reading step can "translate" into a research step. As a class, create a research process that students can refer to over the course of the week.

Teaching Approach

Use of the Handbook

Ask students to spend a few minutes previewing the Reader's Almanac. Have them create a Magnet Summary that explores the various sections of the almanac and how they think they might use them. Ask them to use sticky notes to mark elements that they're unsure about.

Extend the Handbook

Assign a simple research project students can complete over the course of the week. (An example might be to have them find information on one of the authors or selections published in the *Reader's Handbook*.) As a first step, have students set their purpose. Next, they'll want to get a sense of the materials that are available. As a third step, ask them to make a research plan in which they name the reading strategies and tools they'll use and the sources they'll consult.

Assessment

Ask students:

■ What kinds of information are available the Reader's Almanac?

■ How are the reading process and research process similar?

WEEK 34
Lesson 2
Locating Information

For use with *Reader's Handbook* pages 694–705

Goals

In this lesson, students explore the variety of sources available to them for research.

Teaching Focus

Background

Encourage your student researchers to use a *combination* of primary and secondary sources. Explain to the class that a research report based solely on information from primary sources might be questioned for breadth or reliability, while a research report based solely on secondary sources can seem dry and impersonal. Suggest that students strive for a balance when planning what sources they'll use.

Instruction

Discuss research projects students have done in the past and the types of sources they've consulted. Assess their ability to identify appropriate sources for various types of research projects. Use the information in the *Reader's Handbook* to supplement your teaching. Then begin your discussion of primary vs. secondary sources. Explore ways to get the most out of library research and refine students' understanding of how to find information on the Internet.

Teaching Approach

Use of the Handbook

Ask students to read silently pages 694–696. Then walk them through the pages 698–705 on using the library. If you haven't covered it already, read with students key information on using the Internet (see Reading a Website, pages 512–527).

Extend the Handbook

Here students will work on the second part of the research process: read and connect. Have students gather their sources in one place before they do their active readings. Then ask them to read carefully the material they've gathered, taking notes as they go. (Suggest reading tools students might use to keep track of their notes.) When they've finished, have students pair off and discuss what they've found and the connections they were able to make to the subject.

Assessment

Ask students:

■ What is the difference between a primary and a secondary source?

■ What are examples of primary and secondary sources?

■ Why is it important to strike a balance between the two types of sources when conducting research?

WEEK 34
Lesson 3   Evaluating Sources

For use with *Reader's Handbook* pages 706, 757

Goals

Here students explore the importance of and process for evaluating primary and secondary sources.

Teaching Focus

Background

With the proliferation of websites and the increased accessibility of the Internet, students need to learn how to carefully evaluate their reference sources. In the Reading a Website section of the *Reader's Handbook* (pages 512–527), you discussed how to evaluate a website. Take what students learned there and help them apply it to research sources in general. Emphasize the importance of verifying facts and details by checking for the same information in a different source—perhaps even a different *type* of source.

Instruction

Explain that in this lesson students will concentrate on ways they can test a research source for accuracy and reliability. Begin the lesson by asking students why it's important to test the validity of a source. Then point out the Website Profiler on page 757 and compare it to the Source Evaluator shown on page 706. Explain that these two tools can help students decide if the information they've found in their research is trustworthy. Make the point that information that cannot be documented by at least two sources is not considered entirely reliable. Encourage students to double-check the information provided by a primary source with a secondary source.

Teaching Approach

Use of the Handbook

After students examine the Source Evaluator at the bottom of page 706, have them read the text that appears above the organizer. Point out the Checklist for Evaluating a Source and walk through the questions with students. Help students see that these questions can be used with any type of source.

Extend the Handbook

Invite students to create a Source Evaluator for each book, magazine, and website they used for their research projects. Remind students of the importance of eliminating (and perhaps substituting) sources that are not reliable.

Assessment

Ask students:

■ Why is it important to evaluate the reliability of your sources?

■ How can a Source Evaluator help you evaluate sources?

WEEK 34
Lesson 4

Tracking and Documenting Information

For use with *Reader's Handbook* pages 707–712

Goals

Here you'll discuss methods for keeping track of and documenting research.

Teaching Focus

Background

One of the most important aspects of reading actively is taking thoughtful and precise notes. The act of writing while reading can make it easier to process information. The Reading Tools section of the handbook contains a series of organizers that students can use for their research notes. These include Close Reading Organizers, Outlines, Summary Notes, and Cause-Effect Organizers. Draw students' attention to these and other organizers as you discuss note-taking.

Instruction

Ask students to suggest reading tools they might use to keep track of their research notes. Direct their attention to the Note Cards on page 708. Making research notes as complete as possible will help when it comes time to document their sources. Then discuss actual documentation styles and information that is key to both formal and informal documentation. Have on hand copies of *Writers INC* and *The Chicago Manual of Style* for students to glance through when they have time.

Teaching Approach

Use of the Handbook

Ask students to preview pages 707–712. Review the importance of keeping good notes while researching. Then read aloud the Taking Notes section on page 707 and help students examine the sample Note Cards on page 708. Ask a volunteer to explain the difference between quoting and paraphrasing a source. Explain how vital it is to avoid the temptation of plagiarism when researching. Finish the lesson with a discussion of documentation styles and your expectations for students documenting sources for your class.

Extend the Handbook

Have students present their research in the form of a mini written report or 60-second oral presentation. Remind students that their final product should include only the most important facts and that each of these facts should be supported. Before their presentations, have students create a bibliography of sources.

Assessment

Ask students:

■ What are some good note-taking tools that can make your job as researcher easier?

■ What is plagiarism and how can you avoid it?

213

WEEK 35

Strategy Handbook

For use with *Reader's Handbook* pages 713–737

Daily Lessons	Summary
Lesson 1 **Strategy Overview**	Present an overview of the Strategy Handbook. Discuss its purposes and uses.
Lesson 2 **Close Reading and Note-taking**	Review and refine students' understanding of two important strategies: close reading and note-taking.
Lesson 3 **Skimming and Summarizing**	Enhance students' knowledge of skimming and summarizing. Model how to use the strategies with fiction and nonfiction.
Lesson 4 **Synthesizing**	Further students' understanding of the strategy of synthesizing and how it can strengthen their understanding of a text.

Lesson Resources

See *Teacher's Guide* pages 432–440.

See Website www.greatsource.com/rehand

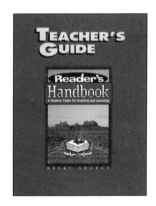

Reading Tools

For use with *Reader's Handbook* pages 738–757

Daily Lessons	**Summary**
Lesson 1 **Before Reading Tools**	Build an understanding of the various tools students can use as preparation for reading a text.
Lesson 2 **During Reading Tools**	Explore reading tools that work well at the During Reading stage of the reading process.
Lesson 3 **After Reading Tools**	Review reading tools students can use to help them reflect upon and respond to a text.
Lesson 4 **The *Reader's Handbook* in Review**	Discuss the skills and strategies students explored in the *Reader's Handbook*. Respond to students' questions, comments, and concerns.

Lesson Resources

Overheads

For this lesson, use:
Overhead 1: The Reading Process

See *Teacher's Guide* pages 441–479.

See Website www.greatsource.com/rehand

WEEK 35
Lesson 1   Strategy Overview

For use with *Reader's Handbook* pages 713–737

Goals

In this lesson, you'll give students a sense of the purpose of the Strategy Handbook and help them identify the strategies they'd like to learn more about.

Teaching Focus

Background

Here you'll discuss with students how they can use the Strategy Handbook to reinforce what they know about the strategies they've used over the course of the year. You might want to identify three or four strategies with which the class is struggling, and then teach a series of lessons on those strategies. What follows is a discussion of five of the more important reading strategies explored in the *Reader's Handbook:* close reading, note-taking, skimming, summarizing, and synthesizing. You can model your own lessons on the ones shown here.

Instruction

As an opening activity, have students preview the Strategy Handbook with sticky notes in hand. Ask them to place sticky notes beside the strategies that they feel they need to work on. When students have finished, make a list of strategies the class wants to focus on and design your week of lessons around them. After reviewing each strategy, have students practice using them with literature from the *Reader's Handbook, Student Applications Book 10,* or the appropriate literature anthology.

Teaching Approach

Use of the Handbook

Have students read the introduction and table of contents to the Strategy Handbook on page 713. Then have them preview the entire section and make notes about strategies they'd like to explore in further detail. (You might have students rate the relative difficulty of these strategies from 1 to 5, with 5 being the most challenging.) Next, take a look at strategies that students feel confident about. Ask them to explain how they plan to use the strategy in the future.

Extend the Handbook

Take this opportunity to review all the strategies listed in the handbook. Divide the class into groups and assign two or more strategies to each group. Have the group read the handbook's discussion of the strategy, and create Key Word or Topic Notes as they read. Topics for the left-hand column of their notes include: Purpose, Definition, Example, Reading Tools, and so on.

Assessment

Ask students:

■ What is the purpose of the Strategy Handbook?

■ How would you explain how to use your favorite strategy?

WEEK 35
Lesson 2

Close Reading and Note-taking

For use with *Reader's Handbook* pages 714–715 and 718–719

Goals

Here you'll reinforce students' understanding of close reading and note-taking.

Teaching Focus

Background

Close reading and note-taking are two of the most important strategies, since they force readers to remain actively involved with the text. In addition, these two strategies help students see that the reader is ultimately responsible for extracting meaning from the text. Close reading means reading line for line, word by word. The strategy works particularly well with short pieces of literature and poetry. Intertwined with close reading is note-taking, a strategy that helps students remember key details from a work. Every reading tool explored in the Reading Tools section supports the strategy of note-taking.

Instruction

Begin by asking students to reflect on the two strategies. Ask them to explain close reading and note-taking without looking at the definitions in the handbook and provide examples if they can. Ask them to name reading tools that work well with the strategies and the type of literature that they best support. Then read with students the handbook discussion of the strategies. Choose a selection from students' literature anthologies and model how to do a close reading.

Teaching Approach

Use of the Handbook

After your general discussion of the strategies, direct students' attention to page 714. Have a volunteer read aloud the Description and then discuss the information about using the strategy as a class. Point out the questions readers might ask themselves as they do their close readings. See if students can add their own questions to the list. Then have them turn to pages 718 and 719. Follow the same steps as before: ask students to define, then read and discuss.

Extend the Handbook

Have students do a close reading of a poem from *Student Applications Book 10* ("The Charge of the Light Brigade," page 152, "The Bells," page 162, or "After Death," page 160.) Have students make their close reading notes in a Double-entry Journal.

Assessment

Ask students:

■ How would you explain the strategy of close reading?

■ What in your opinion is the best way to take notes?

WEEK 35
Lesson 3
Skimming and Summarizing

For use with *Reader's Handbook* pages 728–731

Goals

In this lesson, students will refine their understanding of skimming and summarizing.

Teaching Focus

Background

Skimming and summarizing enable the reader to take an active role in the reading process. Both strategies help foster a deeper understanding of the text in general and the author's thesis or main idea in particular. In this lesson, you'll ask students to explore both strategies in some detail and then practice using them.

Instruction

Begin by reminding students that skimming is an excellent strategy to use with textbooks and tests. Have a volunteer explain the applications of the strategy with these and other types of reading. Be sure to emphasize, however, that skimming is meant to supplement—and not replace—a careful reading of a text. Next, discuss the strategy of summarizing. Ask students to explain the difference between summarizing and paraphrasing. Be sure students understand that summarizing can help a reader sort important from unimportant details in a reading. End with a discussion of how the two strategies can be used with fiction and nonfiction alike.

Teaching Approach

Use of the Handbook

Read aloud or have a student read aloud the top of pages 728–729. Do the same for the strategy of summarizing (pages 730–731). Ask half the class to skim a newspaper or magazine article using an Outline (see page 749) for their notes. Have the other half of the class read and then summarize the same articles on Summary Notes. If you'd like all students to work from the same article, have them use "Two Inmates Vanish from Alcatraz" on pages 76–78 of *Student Applications Book 10*.

Extend the Handbook

Ask students to thumb through the Reading Tools section of the handbook and search for two or more tools that they think work particularly well with the strategies of skimming and summarizing. Discuss as a class.

Assessment

Ask students:

■ What is the purpose of skimming and how does it differ from summarizing?

■ What should you look for when summarizing fiction? When summarizing nonfiction?

218

WEEK 35
Lesson 4 — Synthesizing

For use with *Reader's Handbook* pages 732–733

Goals

Here you'll encourage students to reflect upon the strategy of synthesizing and how they can use it to help them get more from fiction and nonfiction texts alike.

Teaching Focus

Background

Synthesizing can be a difficult reading strategy for students to master, although many readers synthesize without even realizing it. You might use a jigsaw puzzle analogy as a way of helping students understand that a book, article, or story has individual pieces that can be examined on their own. Also ask them to think about how much more complete (and interesting) a puzzle is each time a new piece is added. The same is true for synthesizing literary or structural elements in a text.

Instruction

Ask volunteers to explain what it means to "synthesize." Lead students to understand that synthesizing means examining the different parts of a text on their own and then putting them back together to see a cohesive whole. Point out that synthesizing works with nonfiction as well as fiction and have students discuss possible examples. Then turn to the information in the Strategy Handbook. Indicate the Fiction Organizer at the bottom of page 732 and explain how it supports the strategy. Have students thumb through the Reading Tools section to find another type of organizer that could help them synthesize nonfiction texts.

Teaching Approach

Use of the Handbook

Ask students to read independently the information on synthesizing on pages 732–733 in the handbook. Then reconvene as a class and discuss the formal definition of the strategy (page 733) and the description offered (page 732).

Extend the Handbook

Ask students to apply the reading strategy of synthesizing to a short passage of their choice. (Have them look for selections in the *Reader's Handbook* or *Student Applications Book 10.)* After completing the activity, have students reflect on the strategy in their journals. Ask them to consider these questions: How would I rate my understanding of synthesizing? Is this a strategy I will use often? Why or why not? What can I do to improve my understanding of the strategy?

Assessment

Ask students:

■ What is synthesizing?

■ How is synthesizing like putting together a jigsaw puzzle?

Before Reading Tools

WEEK 36
Lesson 1

For use with *Reader's Handbook* pages 738–757

Goals

In this lesson, students will explore various fiction and nonfiction reading tools they can use at the Before Reading stage.

Teaching Focus

Background

The Reading Tools section of the handbook is a glossary of the 38 tools and organizers presented in the *Reader's Handbook*. There are many different ways you can explore this section, including teaching mini-lessons on different tool groupings (such as those that support fiction, those that support textbooks, those that support poetry, and so on) or focusing on just one or two key tools and inviting students to create their own versions. This lesson and the two that follow provide a general overview of tools that can be used at the Before, During, and After Reading stages. Remind students that most of the tools in the handbook can be adapted at any stage of the reading process and any type of text.

Instruction

Have students recall and reflect upon the reading tools they've been using with the *Reader's Handbook*. Ask them to write as many as they can think of in their journals. Next to the name of each tool, students should write its purpose. Then discuss students' lists as a class. Divide the board into three sections: Before, During, and After Reading. Have students help you sort the tools into the categories. Point out that some tools (such as a Web, for example) may work at all three stages of the reading process. Be sure that students include Magnet Summaries, Preview Charts, Outlines, Setting Charts, and Webs.

Teaching Approach

Use of the Handbook

Have students look at the table of contents for the Reading Tools section on page 738. Then have them read the appropriate pages for the tools they listed on the board. Be sure students notice the handbook page references that accompany each tool description. Refer to these pages to see how the tool is used with text.

Extend the Handbook

Ask students to choose a novel from your classroom library and then preview the book. (Direct them to the Preview Checklist on page 289 if you feel they need it.) Have students write their preview notes on a Preview Chart or Web.

Assessment

Ask students:

■ What are the best tools to use in the Before Reading stage of the reading process?

■ What is a Preview Chart and how does it work?

220

WEEK 36
Lesson 2 — During Reading Tools

For use with *Reader's Handbook* pages 738–757

Goals

Here students explore the reading tools that work well at the During Reading stage.

Teaching Focus

Background

The great majority of the reading tools listed in the Reader's Almanac can be used at the During Reading stage of the reading process. Cause-Effect Organizers, Classification Notes, and 5 W's and H Organizers, among others, can be used to support the Read with a Purpose step, while Critical Reading Charts, Double-entry Journals, and Making Connections Charts work well with the Connect step. Key here is for students to choose the organizers that work best for them.

Instruction

Explain to students that in this lesson they'll be exploring reading tools they can use at the During Reading stage of the reading process. (To help students get a handle on the material, you might further divide this category into subgroups: During Reading tools for fiction and During Reading tools for nonfiction.) Tell the class that you'd like them to become expert users of two different During Reading tools. Allow them to choose their own tools, with the proviso that they choose one for fiction and one for nonfiction. Have them read about the tool in Reading Tools and then turn to the examples in the handbook.

Teaching Approach

Use of the Handbook

Once again, direct students' attention to page 738. Walk through the list of tools as a class and discuss which tools work best with fiction and which with nonfiction. Draw students' attention to several that you think they will use most often, including the Character Map, Critical Reading Chart, Double-entry Journal, Fiction Organizer, Main Idea Organizer, Plot Diagram, Sequence Notes, and Venn Diagram. Direct students to read the text that supports each tool and then create their own version of one or two organizers.

Extend the Handbook

Have students reread a fiction or nonfiction selection from *Student Applications Book 10* and then choose a reading tool to create notes about the text. Ask several students to share their work with the class.

Assessment

Ask students:

■ How can using reading tools help you become a more active reader?

■ What are the best reading tools to use with fiction?

WEEK 36
Lesson 3
After Reading Tools

For use with *Reader's Handbook* pages 738–757

Goals

Here students explore tools they can use with the After Reading stage of the reading process.

Teaching Focus

Background
At the After Reading stage, readers reflect upon, make inferences about, and evaluate a text. It's difficult to accomplish all of these things without some type of organizer. Here you'll review with students the features of several reading tools that can help get the job done.

Instruction
Return to the board for a final Reading Tools activity. In the After Reading section, make a list of tools and organizers students feel are appropriate to use at this point in the reading process. (Students might suggest Argument Charts, Main Idea Organizers, Making Connections Charts, Paraphrase or Retelling Charts, Source Evaluators, Topic and Theme Organizers, and Website Profilers, among others.) When students finish brainstorming, divide them into small groups and assign two or more tools to each group. Ask group members to read the information in the handbook, explore any questions they have, and then create their own versions of the tools. When all groups have finished, discuss their work.

Teaching Approach

Use of the Handbook
Have a volunteer review the steps of the After Reading stage of the reading process. Invite others to recall After Reading organizers they've used over the course of the year with the *Reader's Handbook* and *Student Applications Book 10.* Ask students, Which tools work best with fiction? Which work best with nonfiction? Label each tool listed on the board as *F, N,* or *B* for *both*. Explain that students may want to change these designations after they read the Reading Tools text.

Extend the Handbook
Ask students to re-apply the After Reading stage of the reading process to one of the selections in the handbook or *Applications Book.* Have them go through each step of the process, using one or more reading tools to record their ideas.

Assessment
Ask students:

■ How can reading tools best help you at the After Reading stage of the reading process?

■ Which tools do you see yourself using most consistently with future readings?

■ Which reading tools work best for you in the After Reading stage?

WEEK 36
Lesson 4

The *Reader's Handbook* in Review

For use with the *Reader's Handbook* as a whole

Goals

Here you'll encourage students to reflect upon the work they've done this year in the *Reader's Handbook*.

Teaching Focus

Background

At the start of the year, students previewed the *Reader's Handbook* as a whole and then made note of their personal goals for reading. Use this final lesson as a way of reviewing what students learned and reflecting upon how well they have met their original purposes for reading the handbook.

Instruction

Begin by reiterating that reading is a process, and as such it is constantly evolving. The more a reader reads, the more proficient he or she becomes. With proficiency comes enjoyment, which is why students who read most often seem to derive the most satisfaction from a variety of texts. Then ask students to think about the goals they set at the beginning of the year, and decide which of these they were able to meet. End the lesson with a discussion of how students can use what they've learned from the *Reader's Handbook* in their other work in high school.

Teaching Approach

Use of the Handbook

As a group, read and then discuss the goals listed on pages 16–18 of the handbook. Was the class able to meet most of these goals? Why or why not? Then have students reflect silently upon their own goals and think about what they've accomplished. At the end of the lesson, explore the variety of ways students can use the *Reader's Handbook* to help with the reading they do in subsequent years of high school. Ask students, How can the *Reader's Handbook* help you write a novel critique? How can it help you prepare for the SATs or ACTs?

Extend the Handbook

Invite students to write brief reviews of the *Reader's Handbook*. Ask them to open with a summary of what the book is about. Next, they'll state and then support their opinions of the text. Ask them to end their reviews with a recommendation.

Assessment

Ask students:

■ How has your work with the *Reader's Handbook* changed the way you read?

■ What is the most important thing you learned about reading this year?

Lessons Index